Primary
Humanities

Learning through Enquiry

Education at SAGE

SAGE is a leading international publisher of journals, books, and electronic media for academic, educational, and professional markets.

Our education publishing includes:

- accessible and comprehensive texts for aspiring education professionals and practitioners looking to further their careers through continuing professional development

- inspirational advice and guidance for the classroom

- authoritative state of the art reference from the leading authors in the field

Find out more at: **www.sagepub.co.uk/education**

Primary Humanities

Learning through Enquiry

Tony Pickford, Wendy Garner
and Elaine Jackson

Los Angeles | London | New Delhi
Singapore | Washington DC

Los Angeles | London | New Delhi
Singapore | Washington DC

SAGE Publications Ltd
1 Oliver's Yard
55 City Road
London EC1Y 1SP

SAGE Publications Inc.
2455 Teller Road
Thousand Oaks, California 91320

SAGE Publications India Pvt Ltd
B 1/I 1 Mohan Cooperative
Industrial Area
Mathura Road
New Delhi 110 044

SAGE Publications Asia-Pacific Pte Ltd
3 Church Street
#10-04 Samsung Hub
Singapore 049483

Editor: James Clark
Assistant editor: Monira Begum
Production manager: Bill Antrobus
Production editor: Nicola Marshall
Copyeditor: Jennifer Gregory
Proofreader: Caroline Stock
Marketing manager: Catherine Slinn
Cover design: Wendy Scott
Typeset by Kestrel Data, Exeter, Devon
Printed by: MPG Printgroup, UK

MIX
Paper from
responsible sources
FSC
www.fsc.org   FSC® C018575

Library of Congress Control Number: 2012940280

British Library Cataloguing in Publication data

A catalogue record for this book is available from
the British Library

ISBN 978-0-85702-339-1
ISBN 978-0-85702-340-7 (pbk)

CONTENTS

FOREWORD

It gives me great pleasure to write the foreword for *Primary Humanities: Learning Through Enquiry*, having known the authors throughout most of their professional lives. They offer primary school teachers and teacher educators a lively, informed and easy-to-use guide on how to use enquiry-led learning to raise standards in primary history and geography.

Primary Humanities: Learning Through Enquiry is timely in two ways. First, because successful schools and teachers will always be seeking to shape the curriculum to meet the needs of their children within the context of the local community. Second, because governments around the world constantly wish to define curriculum content – the 'what' that is to be taught – and then generally leave it to schools to identify the 'how', the processes that they might use to achieve this. By developing their own pedagogy, teachers work to provide a challenging and creative education for their learners. It is also hoped that, in the debate, whether at a national, local or school level, is posed the question which is both philosophical and pragmatic, the 'why', as to our reasoning behind the 'what' and the 'how'.

In order to achieve more creative approaches to the curriculum, while at the same time continuing to raise standards of attainment and achievement, teachers and trainee teachers will require reliable advice, ideas and support from a range of sources. This book will provide educators within the primary sector with an avenue of support and reassurance to help them develop a more creative, motivating and challenging enquiry approach.

Over the past 25 years, since the introduction of the National Curriculum in England, there has been broad agreement across all phases of education of the value of enquiry-led learning. It is an approach that is learner-centred and that emphasises higher-order thinking skills. It may take several forms, including analysis, problem solving, discovery and creative activities, both in the classroom and beyond.

In this book, for the first time, all the elements of using the enquiry process are brought together in one place. The authors treat their readers with respect, offering them both the theoretical background and the practical means of putting the theory into action with their learners.

The book helpfully brings together in a single publication the use of enquiry-led learning in both history and geography. This can only be of benefit to both trainee teachers and hard-pressed experienced teachers who, in the primary phase, teach right across the curriculum. The chapters on enquiry outside the classroom and resources to support learning provide information and reassurance to teachers to enable them to gain maximum advantage from an enquiry-led approach. The book also goes well beyond most books on enquiry-led learning in primary schools with its crucially important chapters on progression and assessing progress.

The authors bring their considerable experiences in the classroom as teachers, headteachers, teacher educators and researchers to the task of addressing enquiry-led learning. In short, they can be completely trusted as a reliable source of great ideas, inspiring approaches and unmatched professional knowledge.

Jeremy Krause
Bristol

Jeremy Krause is currently an independent education consultant based in Bristol and Named Trustee of the Geographical Association (GA). He was formerly Senior School Improvement Adviser for the National Strategies in the South West Region, Senior Adviser for Geography Cheshire LA and President of the GA 2001–2.

ABOUT THE AUTHORS

Tony Pickford

After 16 years as a primary school class teacher in Tameside, Manchester, Tony moved into teacher training at the University of Chester to teach on undergraduate and postgraduate programmes. He teaches a range of subjects, including ICT, history and geography education. At various times, Tony has been ICT and research co-ordinator in the Faculty of Education and Children's Services. At the moment, he co-ordinates non-core subjects in the primary programmes and is subject leader for the Global Dimensions specialism. Tony's writing and research interests include intercultural awareness, online learning, e-safety and visual literacy. He is the author or co-author of over 30 articles, book chapters, books and teaching resources. His books for children include the 'What is it Like Now?' series on geography for Key Stage 1 and the 'Children's History of Chester'.

Wendy Garner

Prior to working at the University of Chester, Wendy worked for six years at Hope University, in both the Environmental and Biological Studies Department and the Education Deanery. Wendy was formerly a primary school teacher and geography co-ordinator and has experience of teaching children at Key Stages 1 and 2 of the National Curriculum. She has also worked as an Advisory Teacher in Cheshire and has in the past been a regular provider of lectures and workshops at national and international conferences. Current teaching includes contributions to the Global Dimensions theme and Humanities subjects for BEd/BAQTS primary undergraduates and PGCE primary students. Wendy also teaches on the Education Studies degree route. She is currently in post as Senior Lecturer and Learning, Teaching and Assessment Co-ordinator within the Faculty of Education and Children's Services at the University of Chester.

Elaine Jackson

Elaine has recently taken early retirement from her role as Chief Adviser (Primary) and Joint Head of School Improvement Service for Trafford's Children and Young People's Service. Having qualified with a degree in geography, Elaine followed a PGCE (primary) and then commenced her career in primary education as a teacher, subject co-ordinator, phase manager, deputy head teacher, head teacher, OFSTED inspector and then into the Advisory service. She has experience of teaching in both Key Stages 1 and 2 and also in Early Years Foundation Stage. Over the years, Elaine has contributed to ITT courses, as guest lecturer, at a number of university institutions. She is a regular provider of workshops at local and national conferences and is author of numerous books for children and teachers. Elaine was, for many years, Chair of the Geographical Association's Early Years and Primary Committee (EY and PC) and is currently Chair of Cheshire Development Education Centre (Developing Global Learning).

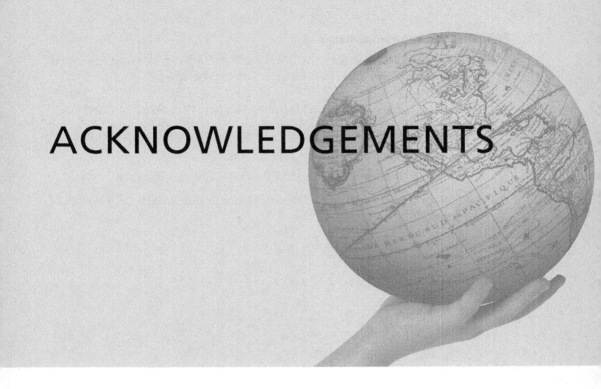

ACKNOWLEDGEMENTS

Author's acknowledgements

The authors would like to thank the following for their contributions to this book:

- Jeremy Krause for the Foreword and his support and inspiration in the past;

- Chris Durbin, Steve Pratchett, Margaret Roberts and Kate Russell for their help and support;

- Sally Davies, Amaryllis Earle, Emma Eastwood and Simon Thomas for case studies;

- Amy and Chloe for drawings of a historian and a geographer; Bryony Freedman and Charlie Wild-Macgregor for help with the drawings;

- Michael O'Sullivan, Michael Glass and Barbara Pickford for their understanding, endurance and patience during the writing process.

Publisher's acknowledgements

SAGE gratefully acknowledges the contributions of the following reviewers who read the proposal and draft chapters along the way:

- Sue Temple, Senior Lecturer in Primary History, University of Cumbria;

- Gill Bivand Taylor, Course Leader Primary Humanities, University of Exeter;

- John Halocha, Bishop Grosseteste University College Lincoln;

- Lynne Dixon, Senior Lecturer, Primary History and Geography, University of Greenwich.

PREFACE

The aim of this book is to introduce, explore and analyse learning and teaching in history and geography through the fundamental processes that underpin learning and practice in these subjects. These processes have been given various labels over time – 'the enquiry process', 'enquiry-led learning', 'the enquiry approach' – with the term 'enquiry' being the key overarching idea and principle. The book begins by exploring what this term means in the context of primary humanities and goes on to analyse how enquiry-based learning may be different in historical and geographical contexts, as well as examine the similarities and commonalities between the subjects.

This book has an explicit and unashamed focus on processes of learning and teaching. This is not to denigrate or downplay the importance of the content of history and geography (although the status of 'facts' is discussed in some depth in Chapter 2), but recognises that children learn best when they are 'doing' history and geography; behaving like historians and geographers to construct knowledge and understandings, rather than being passive receivers of information and 'facts'. If you are looking for a book to give you background knowledge to tell children about Tudor monarchs or coastal erosion, this is not it! There are plenty of reference books, encyclopaedias and online sources you can go to for that. But, if you are looking for a book to help you understand the nature of history and geography in primary education and how you can teach it most effectively, then you have found it. You will find plenty of examples of historical and geographical content knowledge in these pages – content, in the form of examples and case studies, gives context and meaning to the processes of historical and geographical enquiry – but content is a means to an end, not the end point and purpose of primary humanities. This book is about how, by progressing through a range of experiences, resources, settings and contexts, children can become confident, independent and motivated enquirers into historical and geographical questions and issues.

Chapters 3, 4 and 8 explicitly explore contexts for enquiry and the resources on which enquiry is based. Chapter 5 focuses on examples of enquiries from across the primary age range and those seeking ideas and inspiration for translating principles into practice will find plenty to work on here. Chapters 6 and 7 focus on two of the more challenging aspects of learning and teaching: progression and assessment. Both provide timely and refreshing ideas and advice. Progression is explored through children's increasing participation in enquiries and activities as well as a look at alternative models of enquiry. The chapter on assessment looks at generic and humanities-specific issues, but also addresses some of the fundamental ideas and questions about assessment. At a time when the curriculum as a whole seems increasingly assessment-driven and test-orientated, questions such as 'Why assess?' and 'Who for?' need to be asked.

This is fundamentally a book about learning, however – children's learning and your learning as an educator – and there are features throughout the book to develop your understanding of enquiry through reflection, interaction and action.

- You will find short case studies throughout the book, alongside lengthier examples of practice in Chapter 5, which illustrate key points or show resources being used in context. Many of these were written by practising teachers and trainee teachers. Please adapt and develop these ideas for your own use.

- 'To think about' pieces pose questions for reflection or discussion with colleagues.

- 'Try this activity' items suggest activities to try with children or with colleagues.

- 'Useful websites' for online research and resources are also identified throughout the book.

- At the end of each chapter, you will find a short summary paragraph, which highlights the key issues and points that have been covered.

- Also at the end of every chapter, except Chapter 7 on assessment, you will find a list of references. These show the key reading and research evidence on which the chapters are based and will be useful lists for your further research. Chapter 7 provides a list of 'Further reading' for those who wish to explore the key area of assessment in more depth.

Finally, each chapter begins with a set of learning objectives, which outline what you will be able to do after reading the chapter. It may seem something of a contradiction for a book based on constructivist principles to have such behaviourist lists, but objectives have their place, providing they are seen as signposts and starting points, not limits. Our aim is to fire your enthusiasm about enquiry in history and geography, starting you on a journey in which you and the children you teach will go beyond objectives into as yet unplanned and unknown learning experiences prompted by searching questions and unexpected answers.

CHAPTER 1

WHY DO ENQUIRY-LED LEARNING?

By the end of this chapter you will be able to:

- explore the notion of enquiry as a pedagogical approach;
- consider historical perspectives of learning and teaching approaches in humanities;
- relate enquiry to inductive and deductive reasoning;
- consider psychological perspectives and the relationship of enquiry to learning theory;
- analyse relevant research and consider implications for future practice.

Introduction

'Enquiry' is a term which is generally perceived as referring to the process of focused questioning and research. Ultimately this is with a view to reaching a reasoned conclusion, although the process of enquiry itself is also of significance to the learner. Enquiry is an accepted learning and teaching approach within primary history and geography and, as a pedagogical context, there are a number of perspectives from which the notion of enquiry might be explored.

Historically the pedagogical method of enquiry is not new and evidence for the use of enquiry in primary history and geography dates back to at least the early 1900s (Garner, 2007; Collingwood, 1939, as cited in Cooper, 2000: 3). The enquiry method is firmly rooted within psychological theories of learning and this provides a clear rationale for its use within the primary humanities. There is, however, much research to indicate that there is a significant discrepancy between rhetoric and practice. Therefore, within this chapter, all of these perspectives will be explored and analysed and you will be encouraged to take a critical stance.

Historical perspective

It is useful to reflect on how school geography and history have been planned and taught over time, and to discuss the extent to which enquiry methods are really a modern phenomenon or whether such methods have always been a part of humanities curricula.

 Geography in primary schools

Even as far back as the early twentieth century, within a short paper detailing 'what the primary school geography teacher should know and be', it was suggested that the teacher should 'encourage children to talk, and (dangerous as it may seem) to ask questions about the subject' (Unstead, 1928: 315). A similar view was taken within an early experiment in a junior school where pupils were encouraged to undertake independent enquiry. Pupils had to identify a focus for geographical research and were required to use a number of sources to actually present a lesson on their chosen topic to the rest of the class. This was with a view to encouraging the children to take a 'sufficiently *active* part' in the lesson (Cullis, 1919: 27). The project reported a number of benefits, not least in terms of the enthusiasm of those involved. A later study had similar outcomes, finding that the 'class literally teaches itself' when pupils have opportunities to lead research and participate actively in their own learning (Haddon, 1948: 190).

Benefits identified included increased motivation, proficiency in the use of sources and an increase in pupil questioning about geographical topics (Haddon, 1948). Other small-scale experimentation in elementary schools revealed that teaching seemed to be most effective when pupils' work was framed by the teacher but also self-directed in terms of choice of resources and methods of approach (Jones, 1925). The approach detailed in this particular case study is very similar to the model of mediation identifiable within constructivist models of learning and the notion of a 'framed enquiry' which has been presented more recently as an expression of the level of participation of pupil and teacher in school-based learning environments (Roberts,1987, 2003).

The shift away from 'chalk and talk' or highly didactic methods for primary-aged children continued and within a report commissioned by the GA in 1964 (based on the structure of the Hadow Report of 1931), it advised that the 'curriculum . . . be thought of in terms of activity and experience rather than of facts to be stored' (GA, 1964).

The teaching of geography continued to change in this direction from the early 1970s, moving increasingly towards the use of what was known as 'models' and the employment of problem-solving or 'hypothetical' modes of instruction. This gradual change in teaching methods represented a continued shift away from learning geographical facts to learning how to learn and how to be a young geographer.

Reasoning and enquiry in primary humanities

Deductive and inductive reasoning

The notion of 'models', generating and testing models, theories or generalisations, is akin to what is known as inductive and deductive reasoning. That is, types of reasoning which may be used by students or pupils within any line of enquiry. Both forms of reasoning can be used to test or form hypotheses, but in different and distinct ways.

To think about

Key features of 'deductive reasoning'

General to specific

Hypothesis to confirmation or negation of hypothesis

Conclusion (which may be valid or invalid) as the logical consequence of premises/hypotheses

Deductive approach in **geography** is where students generate aims and hypotheses based upon prior theoretical knowledge, then select appropriate methods, collect data and carry out analysis within a specific case study context.

Students choose the cheapest mode of transport when travelling long distances (Premise A)

Travelling by coach is the cheapest mode of travel for travelling long distances (Premise B)

Most students travel by coach when travelling long distances (conclusion based on premises/data analysed)

Deductive approach in **history** is where students generate aims and hypotheses based upon prior theoretical knowledge, then make observations of and analyse sources within a specific case study context.

The use of coal was limited by cost of transportation (Premise A)

Canals reduced the cost of transporting heavy goods (Premise B)

The use of coal rose in areas linked by canals to coal mines (conclusion based on premises/data analysed)

To think about

Key features of 'inductive reasoning'

Specific to general

Hypothesis formulated on basis of data collected; Observation – theory building

Explains relationships between facts and allows predictions of the future through formulation of laws/rules/hypotheses

Inductive approach in **geography** is where we collect first-hand data and then make generalisations/build theory based on this

Collect data about physical features of glaciated valleys in the French Alpine region – make generalisations about features which may be common to all glacial valleys (concepts of patterns and processes)

Inductive approach in **history** is where we make observations from a certain period and then make generalisations about the identified period

Make observations of political documents, letters, census data from the Victorian era – make generalisations about how people lived based on this (concepts of similarity and difference, cause and effect)

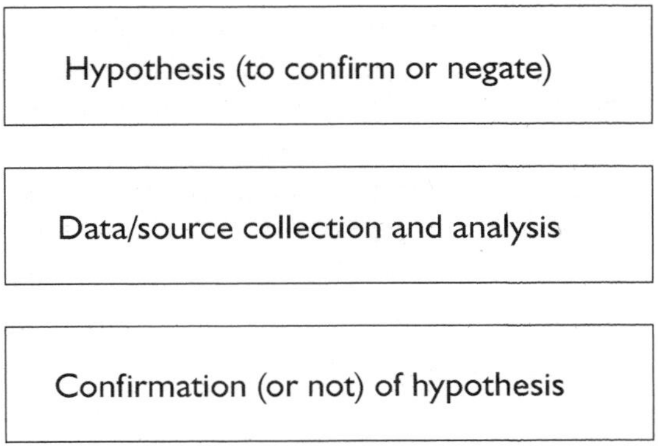

Hypothesis (to confirm or negate)

Data/source collection and analysis

Confirmation (or not) of hypothesis

Figure 1.1 Deductive model

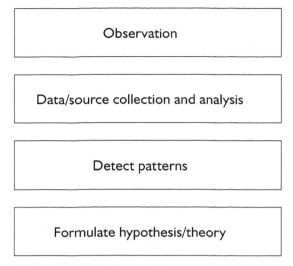

Figure 1.2 Inductive model

There are many advantages of using hypothetical methods of teaching. First, greater intellectual potency can be achieved when children learn to use hypotheses or models to solve problems. There is opportunity for learners to progressively relate new instances to their framework of fundamental ideas, this of course being directly related to the theory of constructivism. The intrinsic reward in terms of success and failure is more about information rather than reward and punishment. In other words, using this method helps children to construct their own learning and to develop confidence in their ability to learn rather than to be faced with an answer which is either simply correct or incorrect.

A further potential advantage, relates to conservation of memory and how 'discovery of things for oneself' (Crisp, 1969: 13) can lead to more personal and relevant storage of cognitive information; that this in turn can facilitate ease of retrieval later. Enhanced levels of motivation and participation of learners, coupled with the development of key and transferable skills, are also arguments in favour of this approach.

The distinction between inductive and deductive reasoning in relation to primary history and primary geography will be explored further within Chapter 2.

Types of reasoning and the enquiry process

In terms of enquiry then, what is the relationship between these types of reasoning and an enquiry-based approach?

As described above, both inductive and deductive reasoning can be classed as hypothetical modes of learning and teaching, the main distinction being where the enquiry begins. With inductive reasoning, an enquiry may start with an observation of a phenomenon which raises questions that then subsequently shape the investigation. Deductive reasoning however, begins with a hypothesis and, through research, the key objective is to confirm or negate the hypothesis.

While starting points are different, the key elements within each process are similar; data/source collection and analysis and hypothesis testing and formulation. These aspects are important features of an enquiry-based approach (see Figure 1.3).

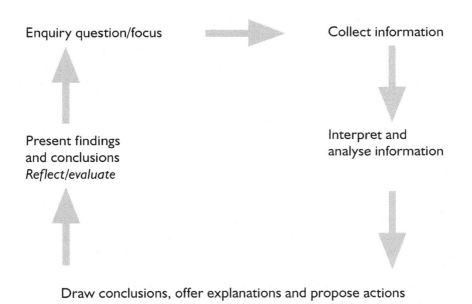

Draw conclusions, offer explanations and propose actions

Figure 1.3 The enquiry process

The enquiry question or focus can be based on inductive or deductive reasoning. For example, in history, the question may be essentially deductive: 'What was domestic life like during the Victorian era? Does the evidence we have support the idea that there was poor sanitation, overcrowding?' By comparison, in geography, the question might be more inductive: 'What is this glaciated valley like?' From this point data may be collected and patterns and processes identified in terms of the character of glacial landscapes. The key point here is that there is a distinction between inductive and deductive reasoning but that both represent key aspects of an enquiry-based approach.

Psychological perspectives

Historical and geographical enquiry is generally perceived as being related to the theory of constructivism. Constructivism is based on the scientific study of mental events in terms of the learner and how the learner uses information to make sense of the world around them. The role of the learner in developing strategies to build knowledge and understanding is central to this theory; it is about how they perceive, interpret, store, retrieve and use information which is critical in effective learning. It is about information and the relationships forged between units of information which leads to the construction of knowledge and understandings.

The implication of this for enquiry is that it should represent a process through which pupils can 'learn about the world by actively making sense of it themselves', in contrast to models of learning where knowledge is seen as being 'transmitted to us ready-made' (Roberts, 2003: 27). Learning is about constructing meaning in relation to what is already known. All learners understand the world in different ways due to varying social and cultural factors and contexts. Because of this phenomenon, new information must be accommodated and assimilated within an individual's existing constructs, as opposed to being 'bolted on' as ready-made knowledge (Barnes and Todd, 1995, as cited by Roberts, 2003).

Two key proponents of this theory of constructivism include Bruner and his notion of *'discovery learning'* and Vygotsky and his model of the *'Zone of Proximal Development'*.

Bruner and enquiry

For Bruner, education and learning is about the construction of our own version of reality through personal experiences and the development of relationships between concepts ('coding systems' or 'categories'). The implication of this for pupils and students in education is that they should not be presented with information in its final form, but that they should be active in processing the information themselves. Because of this, the role of the teacher is not only to impart knowledge but also to guide learners in discovering new knowledge and understandings for themselves.

In terms of enquiry, curriculum models should help to facilitate the development of coding systems through the incorporation of methodologies which will help learners to develop their thinking. Related to this, Bruner describes the 'act of learning' as involving three processes. First, there is 'acquisition' of new information; second, 'transformation' of knowledge; and third 'evaluation' (Bruner, 1977). According to Bruner, after or while the information is being acquired, transformation occurs; transformation is about 'the process of manipulating knowledge to make it fit new tasks' (Bruner, 1977: 48). This refers to the application and development of new and existing knowledge so as to make sense of new facts, problems and issues. Bruner goes on to identify the third process of learning as being 'evaluation' and notes how this essentially refers to the process of reflection on one's learning and the extent to which knowledge has been appropriately applied and manipulated. This tripartite model, although not necessarily sequential (the three processes may be almost simultaneous (Bruner, 1977)), does clearly relate to the models of enquiry and reasoning detailed earlier.

Vygotsky and enquiry

Again, for Vygotsky, education and learning is about the construction of our own knowledge and understanding; it is about developing the knowledge of *how* to write a book as opposed to noting down dictated instructions, verbatim. The role of language and culture is seen as having pivotal significance within this variation of constructivist theory.

Social constructivism, of which Vygotsky is a key proponent, emphasises the significance of others in helping us to understand the world; Vygotsky identifies the 'Zone of Proximal Development' as a model representing the level of achievement that can be reached unaided, compared with the higher levels of achievement facilitated through mediation by teacher or peers.

> the Zone of Proximal Development is . . . the distance between the actual developmental level as determined by independent problem solving and the level of potential development as determined through problem solving under adult guidance or in collaboration with more capable peers.
>
> (Vygotsky, 1978: 86)

   This assistance by others in pupils' learning is often referred to as 'scaffolding' (Daniels, 2001). The teacher (for example) can help 'a child or novice to solve a problem, carry out a task or achieve a goal which would (otherwise) be beyond his unassisted efforts' (Woods (1976) as cited by Daniels, 2001: 107). 'Scaffolding' helps to simplify the role of the learner rather than the task, through structured help by more capable others. It is the difference between learning how to develop a new skill or concept unaided compared with having the opportunity to do this with an appropriate expert or a more knowledgeable other. In short, without language and mediation, the Zone of Proximal Development remains 'untouched' and the shift from elementary to higher-order functioning is not facilitated.

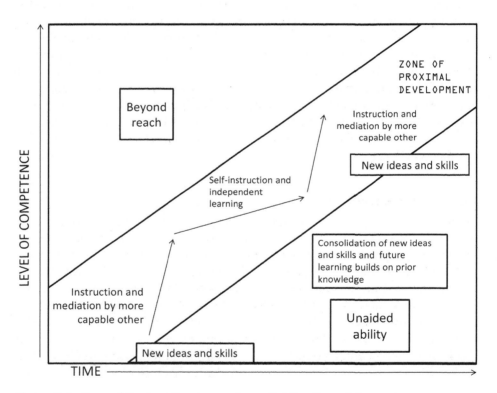

Figure 1.4 Zone of Proximal Development – scaffolding through focused and facilitated enquiry

To think about

What are the implications for the role of the learner and the teacher (or 'expert other') within this model proposed by Vygotsky (see Figure 1.4)?

Think about a time when you have been guided by a more expert learner in your own learning, in such a way that your competence subsequently improved.

What starter activities did the expert use?

How did they continue to instruct and to guide you?

Did they provide you with information?

Did they ask questions and probe for explanations?

Did they correct mistakes and misconceptions?

In terms of what was being learned, how did you make the transition between teacher-assisted and independent learning? At what point did you feel the scaffolding was no longer necessary, and why not?

 Try this activity

With a partner, think about the analogy of using a map to guide you to a specific location. The map provides important directions and information to guide you to your destination and this is similar to the role of the teacher in Vygotsky's model of the Zone of Proximal Development (Figure 1.4). Select a topic for a history- or geography-focused lesson. Note down what starter activities you might use and how you will then go on to instruct and mediate so as to enable the learner to reach improved levels of competence.

In conclusion, the implications of constructivism for pupils, focusing on the work of Bruner and Vygotsky, include the need to take prior learning into account and to provide pupils with the opportunity to relate new knowledge to what is already known. In addition to this, the significance of others in helping to reshape knowledge and understandings should also be taken into account, by both the teacher and the learner.

Thinking skills and enquiry

More recent pedagogical innovations within the geography and history curriculum have focused on 'thinking skills', a movement which really started to have an impact around the 1980s and links to the work of many important pioneers (Feuerstein et al. (1980); Lipman et al. (1980); de Bono (1992). Both the notion of an enquiry process and an increased emphasis on 'thinking skills' represents a shift towards more progressive educational ideology as both aim to develop increased autonomy in learners, as learners.

There is considerable overlap between 'thinking skills' and 'enquiry', and it could be argued that they are, in essence, the same thing, or one a part of the other. However, they are often referred to separately within educational contexts and literature, including curriculum documentation found in schools. As described in Table 1.1, the process of learning and the role of language and discussion are central to both thinking skills and enquiry. This relates directly to the work of Bruner and Vygotsky identified and discussed earlier.

Table 1.1   Thinking skills and enquiry

'Thinking skills' (Feuerstein et al. (1980), Lipman et al. (1980), de Bono (1992))	'Geographical enquiry' (National Curriculum)
Focuses on proces of learning in a way that helps learners to reach higher levels of achievement.	Focuses on the process of learning by following an enquiry route and by reflecting on methods, sources and outcomes in an ongoing way. This process has the potential to inform future enquiries.
'Thinking skills' pioneers stress the importance of language, articulation and discussion ('thinking together').	Within the context of 'geographical enquiry', group work, discussion, reflection and decision making are all identified as important features.

In line with the argument that the boundaries between the two may be artificial, historical and geographical enquiry could be viewed as encompassing all thinking skills, rather than either being a separate entity. Roberts shares this view and critically considers the list of five thinking skills within the context of the National Curriculum:

> What is odd about the list is that all the other skills listed – information processing, reasoning, creative thinking and evaluation – are all needed for different aspects of enquiry work. Enquiry skills are not a sub set of thinking skills, enquiry includes them all.
>
> (Roberts, 2003: 24)

Blooms et al. and enquiry

The process of enquiry can be justified in relation to theories of learning relating to constructivism and particularly because enquiry focuses on the higher-order thinking skills within the cognitive domain as identified by Blooms et al. (1956).

Anderson and Krathwohl (2000) have made some minor but important modifications to this model. Of note here is a significant shift from the use of nouns (as originally used by Blooms et al.) to verbs, implying that learning within the cognitive domains is active in an ongoing way.

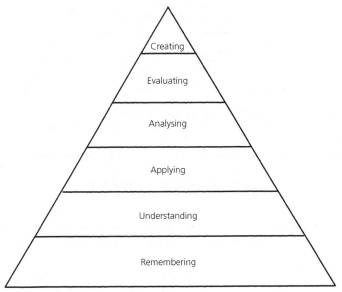

Figure 1.5   Taxonomy of cognitive domains

Source: Based on Anderson (2001) after Blooms et al. (1956)

> ☁ **To think about**
>
> Critically reflect on Blooms et al. and Anderson's taxonomy of cognitive domains (Figure 1.5).
>
> Is the hierarchy appropriate?
> Are skills more important than facts?

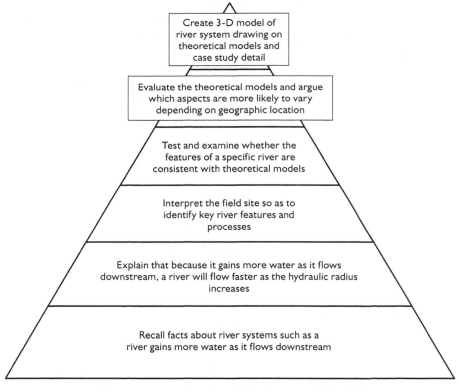

Figure 1.6 Taxonomy of cognitive domains as applied to humanities education

Figure 1.7   Taxonomy of cognitive domains as applied to humanities education

 Try this activity

With a partner, analyse Figures 1.6 and 1.7. Select a history- or geography-focused lesson or concept and map the progression onto Blooms et al. and Anderson's model.

How does this relate to types of reasoning and enquiry, as explored earlier within this chapter?

What are the implications for classroom practice?

What mechanisms need to be in place to ensure progression?

Enquiry-based learning relates to this model proposed by Blooms et al. and Anderson. As it is not only about focusing on the relatively low-status activities of the process of knowledge acquisition, an enquiry approach should facilitate the development of deeper understandings, the ability to apply and analyse information, and to synthesise and evaluate. All of these more complex and advanced levels of cognitive activity are seen as key in helping the pupil to reach higher levels of achievement.

Research into practice

Research into perceptions of enquiry and how enquiry might manifest itself as a learning and teaching approach in the classroom environment was explored by Garner in 2007. Responses from a survey of Initial Teacher Training Tutors from across a number of institutions were used to generate a shared view of an 'Ideal Enquiry-based Learning Task'. The 'Ideal Enquiry-based Learning Task Inventory' (IELTI) was administered electronically by e-mail and a total of 15 out of 40 academics responded. This gave an acceptable response rate of 37.5 per cent (Tilley and Norton, 1998; Garner et al., 2002). The process of content analysis was used to identify, hone and merge categories so as to arrive at the composite view shown in Table 1.2.

It is clear from these findings that the perception of an Ideal Enquiry-based Learning Task (IELT) is that it will facilitate autonomous learning and present children with opportunities to ask and answer geographical and historical questions. Usually, the task will be based on a number of stages within the enquiry cycle which comprise asking questions, collecting, recording, analysing, discussing data and drawing conclusions. Evaluation and reflection of the planned enquiry will also feature. The task will have a clear purpose which is meaningful and motivating to pupils. It will be well conceived in terms of exploiting opportunities to develop other aspects of humanities education and knowledge skills, understandings, attitudes and values across the whole curriculum. The task will involve the use of a wide range of high-quality geographical resources and, ideally, will involve some fieldwork and use of artefacts. Children will have the opportunity to work collaboratively and, in planning the task, prior knowledge and varying levels of ability will be taken into account.

Table 1.2   Ideal Enquiry-based Learning: composite view of Initial Teacher Training Tutors (Garner, 2007)

Rank order (based on response frequency)	An Ideal Enquiry-based Learning Task
1	The task facilitates autonomous learning – opportunities to ask and answer geographical/historical questions – and fosters creativity;
2	The task is based on the 'enquiry cycle', i.e. ask, plan, collect/record/analyse/discuss data and sources, make deductions, draw conclusions, evaluate, identify further questions, etc. (comprising some higher-order thinking skills/reflection);
3	The task has a clear purpose which is meaningful and motivating to pupils;
= 4	The task connects with other aspects of humanities teaching and cross-curricular concepts and skills – including development of attitudes and values;
= 4	The task involves the use of a wide range of good-quality geographical and historical resources and sources;
=4	The task involves fieldwork and artefacts/objects (including buildings) as appropriate;
5	The task is organised as a collaborative group activity;
6	The task takes prior geographical and/or historical knowledge into consideration and differentiation is appropriate.

To think about

Reflection: Implications for practice

Taking a critical stance, and given what you have read, what are the implications for your classroom practice with specific reference to the following:

?   The quality of questioning and role of the teacher;
?   The unique child and prior learning;
?   The curriculum contexts in which enquiry approaches may be used – time frames, structures and feasibility;
?   The opportunity for creativity;
?   The significance of resourcing and learning outside the classroom;
?   The role of enquiry in engagement, self-esteem, motivation and attainment;
?   The role of enquiry in lifelong learning and the development of key and transferable skills.

☐ Summary

The enquiry approach can be justified in relation to theories of learning (constructivism), particularly because enquiry focuses on the higher-order thinking skills within the cognitive domain (as identified by Blooms et al., 1956) and therefore has the potential to lead to improved gains in achievement.

The composite view of an IELT presented within the latter section of this chapter, based on the responses of ITT tutors, presents a definition of enquiry from a practitioner perspective which can be justified in relation to the literature. The features of the IELT described here relate not only to good practice in humanities teaching as documented from a historical perspective, but also closely to learning theory and, in particular, constructivism.

The challenge for the teacher of primary humanities is to consider how these theoretical and research perspectives apply to learning and teaching with young children and how and when these approaches might be best applied and managed. The following chapters will explore these aspects further and in greater depth.

References

Anderson, J. and Krathwohl, D. (eds) (2000) *A Taxonomy for Learning, Teaching and Assessing; A Revision of Blooms' Taxonomy of Educational Objectives*. London: Pearson.

Blooms, B.S., Engelhart, M.D., Furst, E.J., Hill, W.H. and Krathwohl, D.R. (1956) *Taxonomy of educational objectives: the classification of educational goals; Handbook I: Cognitive Domain*. USA: Longman.

Bruner, J. (1977) *The Process of Education*. USA: Harvard University Press.

Cooper, H. (2000) *The Teaching of History in Primary Schools,* 3rd edn. London: David Fulton.

Crisp, J.A.A. (1969) 'New approaches to teaching geography', *Geography*, 54(1): 11–17.

Cullis, O.M. (1919) An experiment in junior school work', *The Geographical Teacher*, 10(1): 27.

Daniels, H. (2001) *Vygotsky and Pedagogy*. London: Routledge Falmer.

De Bono, E. (1992) *Teaching Your Child to Think.* London: Penguin.

Eliot Hurst, H. (1995) 'Geography has neither existence nor future', in R.J. Johnson, *The Future of Geography*. London: Blackwell, pp. 32–46.

Feuerstein, R., Hoffman, M.B. and Miller, R. (1980) *Instrumental Enrichment: an intervention programme for cognitive modifiability*. Baltimore, USA: University Park Press.

Garner, W.P. (2007) Unpublished thesis, available at: http://chesterrep. openrepository.com/cdr/handle/10034/97297

Garner, W.P., Norton, L.S., Asquith, S., Beaumont, A. and Caldecott, S. (2002) *The distance learning task as a pedagogical context*, in Institute for Learning and Teaching (ILT), *Conference proceedings from the 9th Improving Student Learning Symposium*. Oxford: Oxford Brookes University Press, pp. 247–57.

Geographical Association (1964). 'Geography teaching in primary education: a memorandum', *Geography*, 49(4): 410–15.

Ginsberg, H.P. and Opper, S. (1988) *Piaget's Theory of Intellectual Development*. USA: Prentice Hall.

Haddon, J. (1948) 'An experiment in teaching geography', *Geography*, 33(4): 190–93.

Jones, E.W. (1925) 'Results of experiments in teaching geography in elementary schools', *The Geographical Teacher*, 13(1): 64.

Lipman, M., Sharp, A. and Oscanyan, F. (1980) *Philosophy in the Classroom*. Princeton, USA: Temple University Press.

Marwick, A. (2001) *The New Nature of History: Knowledge, Evidence, Language*. Hampshire: Palgrave.

Norton, L.S., Morgan, K. and Thomas, S. (1995) 'The Ideal Self Inventory: A new measure of self esteem', *Counselling Psychology Quarterly*, 8(4): 305–10.

Roberts, M. (1987) 'Teaching styles and strategies', in A. Kent, D. Lambert, M. Naish and F. Slater (eds) *Viewpoints on teaching and learning: geography in education*. Cambridge, UK: Cambridge University Press, pp. 231–59.

Roberts, M. (2003) *Learning through Enquiry*. Sheffield: Geographical Association.

Tilley, A. and Norton, L.S. (1998) 'Psychology lecturers' conceptions of the ideal student using the Ideal Self Inventory (ISI)', *Psychology Teaching Review*, 7(1): 14–23.

Unstead, J.F. (1928) 'The primary school geography teacher: what should he know and be?', *Geography*, 14(4): 315–22.

Vygotsky, L.S. (1978) *Mind in Society*. USA: Harvard University Press.

CHAPTER 2

WHAT IS ENQUIRY-LED LEARNING IN PRIMARY HISTORY AND GEOGRAPHY?

By the end of this chapter you will be able to:

- explain some similarities and differences between the enquiry processes in history and geography;
- describe the nature and status of facts, interpretations, sources and myths in history and geography;
- describe the implications for teaching and learning of historical and geographical enquiry processes.

This chapter will explore the distinctive features of the enquiry processes in history and geography. In doing so, it will also reveal the links and similarities which give cohesion to the humanities. The starting point, however, needs to be an understanding of what history and geography are like as subjects in the primary school. Although all versions of the National Curriculum have weighed both subjects down with large amounts of content knowledge to be taught, they have also defined processes to be actively experienced and skills to be developed. Children are expected to learn history and geography by *doing* history and geography, not by being passive recipients of imparted knowledge about the past and the world around them. That is not to say, of course, that a didactic approach has no place at all among the range of teaching strategies that may be used in the humanities. Explanation, information-giving and storytelling have key roles in both subjects, not as ends in themselves, but as tools for stimulating and developing enquiries.

The idea of children doing history and geography by *behaving* like historians and geographers is central to an understanding of the subjects in the context of primary education. Of course, such an assertion begs the question: what do historians and geographers *do*? And how does *behaving* like a geographer or an historian relate to enquiry-led learning?

 Try this activity

Draw a historian or a geographer

What do children think historians and geographers look like? You may be familiar with Chambers' 'Draw-A-Scientist Test (DAST)' (1983), which was developed to reveal children's perceptions about scientists. *Wikipedia* has a comprehensive section about it and the ways it has been used by hundreds of researchers to investigate stereotypical views about science and scientists. The most widely studied variable has been gender and it is notable that, over the 30 years that the test has been used in many countries, children's views of scientists as being overwhelmingly male have shown little change.

So, what stereotypical views, if any, do children have about historians and geographers and what they do? Use the DAST methodology to reveal the views and perceptions of children you are working with. Symington and Spurling's (1990) prompt – 'Do a drawing which tells what you know about . . . and their work' – is a good starting point. Do children perceive historians and geographers, just as they do scientists, to be mainly male? What sorts of objects surround historians or geographers? Is the stereotypical historian a balding elderly male in a room full of cobwebby books studying some ancient document with a magnifying glass? Is a geographer depicted as an explorer in a remote environment with map and compass?

A DAHT or DAGT can be very revealing, showing that even children in Key Stage 1 can have some quite stereotypical views about history and geography. If children perceive history and geography as being mainly male domains, how can we make them inclusive for both boys and girls?

You might have a go at drawing a historian or geographer yourself. What stereotypical views do you have about what practitioners in the humanities look like and do? How do these perceptions affect the way in which you might approach the teaching of enquiry in history or geography? In the next section we will look at what it means to 'do' history and geography. After reading it, look again at your stereotypical historian or geographer and see if your perceptions have changed.

Figure 2.1   A historian by Amy, aged 11

Because it has been the subject of explicit academic and philosophical study for many years, discussion about the nature of history, and therefore what historians do, can be accessed fairly straightforwardly. In *The Idea of History* (1946), R.G. Collingwood laid down many of the foundations of history as a modern discipline by rejecting a scientific, fact-based explanatory model. Instead he proposed that history is as much about now as it is about the past, in that historians use interpretation, based on interpolation and

Figure 2.2 A geographer by Chloe, aged 11

imagination, to make inferences based on the evidence of sources that remain. It is not an experimental or scientific approach, but one built on deductive reasoning and a developing understanding of human actions and motivations. Evidence, particularly from the distant past, may be limited and fragmentary, so interpolation is the process by which historians move from what is known to what can be reasonably believed, based on the evidence. Historical imagination is key – making history a genuinely creative subject. It is a particular kind of imagination, however, which Collingwood describes in some detail in *The Idea of History*:

> The historian's picture of his subject, whether that subject be a sequence of events or a past state of things, thus appears as a web of imaginative construction stretched between certain fixed points provided by the statements of his authorities [*the evidence*]; and if these points are frequent enough and the threads spun from each to the next are constructed with due care, always by the *a priori* imagination and never by merely arbitrary fancy, the whole picture is constantly verified by appeal to these data, and runs little risk of losing touch with the reality it represents.

(Collingwood, 1946: 242)

Historical imagination is *a priori* in nature – based on deductive reasoning and knowledge of cause and effect. This makes it no less creative, however, but an imagination that operates within the constraints of rationality and logic. History is, therefore, not a static discipline, but one that grows through the discovery of more evidence (sometimes, from other disciplines) and through the changing and differing perspectives of historians. Differing interpretations will arise through the creative application of historical imagination by different historians. Providing the interpretations make rational and logical links between sources, that take into account understandings about human motivation and aspiration, they will be defensible and valid.

 To think about

Historical imagination

Historical imagination raises two key caveats for historical enquiry in primary schools, especially in the context of work with young children. It demands a sophisticated understanding of why and how people behave, as well as an ability to think inside the mindset of people in the past, who may have had quite a different world view to our own. The so-called 'Gunpowder Plot' of 1605 has been a staple in the Key Stage 1 curriculum for many years and it illustrates very well these issues of historical imagination. To make sense of the evidence about the plot and understand the motivations of the plotters, children will need insights into the strength of their religious beliefs and the profound sense of betrayal that they felt when faced with the policies of King James I. Similarly, the idea of a cellar beneath the House of Lords being rented out and remaining unsearched for days, prior to an event like the State Opening of Parliament, seems ludicrous from a modern perspective. How children can be supported and their learning scaffolded so that they might cope with these imaginative leaps are not the concern of this chapter, but it is clear that historical imagination raises problems as well as creative opportunities.

The imaginative and conjectural nature of historical enquiry provides a key contrast with the enquiry process in geography. Some aspects of geography lend themselves to scientific approaches and constructs. In physical geography, landforms, such as dunes and slopes, can be observed, measured and tested first-hand. In human geography, opinions and views about issues can be gathered through interviews and surveys. Although a fair test is not easy to apply outside of a laboratory, the relative accessibility of evidence makes geography less conjectural and speculative than history. Geographical enquiry can have imaginative elements, of course. It would be impossible to investigate questions about distant localities or environmental developments, for example, without resort to imagination. Key questions about what it might feel like to be in a rainforest or a desert require an ability to visualise. Objectors to wind farm developments protest because they imagine how a cherished landscape will be transformed after turbines have been installed. Geographical imagination is not central to *doing* geography, however, and though it can be a predictive process, geographical enquiry is not fundamentally about *a priori* imagination.

Collingwood's analysis is very much about *doing* history. Philosophically, he does not separate history from the work of historians, but portrays the discipline as a developing process: a human enquiry into past thought and action that is undergoing constant change and flux, through imaginative interpretation. It would be wrong to pretend, however, simply because it fits so readily into an enquiry-focused analysis, that Collingwood's view has not been without its critics. In his article 'Collingwood's Dialectic of History' (1968), Mink addresses the key criticisms of Collingwood's philosophical approach to history, notably his apparent disregard for historical facts, particularly facts of natural events from the past. For Collingwood, history is about reconstructing human thought and action through empathetic imagination. Facts only have relevance in their impact on human thought and their effects on human conduct, discerned by interpretation. To argue that certain facts exist outside the process of history is to misunderstand the nature of the subject. A fact about a natural event, such as a volcanic eruption in the past, is only meaningful through interpretation of the evidence of its human impact and context.

The notion of historical facts and the concept of history as a litany of events and dates still remain attractive ideas to some, however. When the History Working Group was preparing the first version of the National Curriculum for history in 1990, a fierce debate arose about the nature of the subject – a debate that got as far as questions being asked on the floor of the House of Commons. During Prime Minister's Questions in March, a colleague asked the then Prime Minister Margaret Thatcher: 'Why cannot we go back to the good old days when we learnt by heart the names of the kings and queens of England, the names of our warriors and battles and the glorious deeds of our past?' Mrs Thatcher replied by stating: 'What children should be taught in history is the subject of vigorous debate – I agree with him. Children should know the great landmarks of British history and should be taught them at school.'

Speaking at a conference on the teaching of history held by the Institute of Historical Research in 2005, David Starkey, a popular television historian, declared, 'The skills-based approach to the teaching of history is a catastrophe.' Not only is it, in his opinion, wasteful of children's time, it leads to an overly critical and relativistic approach. He blames, not Collingwood, but E.H. Carr, author of *What is History?* (1961), as being responsible for prioritising 'the historian over history and method over content' (Starkey, 2005). In December 2009, the Campaign for Real Education, a pressure group on the political right with a preference for traditional teaching methods, produced a curriculum for primary history that is a list of supposedly uncontested facts to be learned by children, beginning with prehistory and dinosaurs in Year 1 and concluding with medieval kings and queens in Year 6.

In *The New Nature of History* (2001), Marwick is utterly dismissive about the notion of facts. He describes the idea of historical facts as 'ridiculously simplistic'. History is about knowledge based on evidence. He explicitly stresses that historians *do* history and goes on to define what this might mean, by stating:

> 'History' embraces: the writings of historians; the research activities which lie behind these writings; the teaching and learning of both methods, on the one side, and ideas and information on the other; the communication of historical knowledge by various means; all the activities associated with the learning outcomes inherent in the discipline of history.
>
> (p. 31)

It is an all-encompassing definition, which rejects the view that historical enquiry can be separated from history itself – that there are historical facts that can be distinguished from the work of historians. For Marwick, history is a process by which knowledge is generated from evidence, with analysis of primary source material (the relics and traces left by past societies) being central. The work of historians (the secondary sources) provides the narratives, links and connections between primary sources that help us make sense of the past. Marwick is particularly scathing about the view that the distinction between primary and secondary sources is ambiguous. Primary sources are those generated in the period being studied and secondary sources are the work of historians – though he does concede that a secondary source from the 19th century may be considered a primary source by some 21st-century historians because it will give insights into the perspectives and values of the time.

The nature, quantity and veracity of sources throw up another contrast with geographical enquiry. At its simplest level, it is a contrast between the fragmentary traces and relics that historians work with and the plethora of reliable sources available to geographers. This can be a simplistic analysis, however, as some historical events and developments have generated a wealth of reliable, but contradictory sources and some geographical enquiries must rely on a small number of highly contentious pieces of evidence. The events known as '9/11' are a case in point for historians – all manner of reliable, eyewitness accounts are available, but the abundance of conspiracy theories attest to the fact that the evidence can be construed in many different ways. Similarly, the bureaucrats of the Nazi Third Reich were notable for their generation of paperwork to document the actions of the regime. The sheer quantity of material can lead to many different interpretations, however, and the apparent absence of clear documentation in some areas has fostered the bizarre views of Holocaust deniers. In geography, issues surrounding local developments are often informed by a few, very biased sources – the location of a proposed Gypsy Traveller site, for example, will often be the subject of heated, but ill-informed debate. Illegal immigration and its effect on populations has become a particularly contentious issue with a limited evidence base in terms of statistics – critics and conspiracy theorists may talk of cover-ups and plots, but the simple truth is that the clandestine and illicit nature of activities makes the compilation of reliable statistics an impossibility.

In history, the status of primary and secondary sources is clear (at least, according to Marwick), but in geography there is no clear dichotomy. Geographers must analyse and evaluate their sources, without the help of a clear separation between primary and secondary materials. The debate about climate change has been muddied by supposed manipulation of evidence and blurring of the line between scientific data and biased information. Similarly, the issue of food miles – the distance food is transported from the time of its production until it reaches the consumer – is informed by a wealth of statistics about carbon footprints, transport, energy and environmental costs, mostly coming from vested interests. A 2007 study by Lincoln University in New Zealand, for example, found that 2,849 kg of carbon dioxide is produced for every tonne of lamb raised in Britain, while just 688 kg of the gas is released by the production of imported New Zealand lamb, even after it has travelled the 11,000 miles to Britain. Such a startling statistic seems to turn the issue of food miles on its head, raising all sorts of questions for the geographer about the green credentials and economics of locally produced food. The research was widely reported in the press at the time and used by some commentators to deride proponents of local sourcing. A look at Lincoln University's website raises questions, however, in that the Research Centre that produced the research appears to have close links with agricultural organisations and pressure groups, such as *DairyNZ*, which describes itself as representing New Zealand farmers, 'to protect and advance their competitive edge on the global market' (*DairyNZ*, 2010). A news item from February 2007 reported that the lead author of the study was an invited guest at a government-supported event – a barbecue sponsored by the New Zealand meat industry – to mark the 125th anniversary of the departure of the first shipment of frozen meat from New Zealand to Britain. This is not to suggest that the research is flawed or the statistics biased, but setting the study in context illustrates clearly that a separation of geographical sources into primary and secondary types is impossible. The analysis of the carbon footprints of meat production in New Zealand and the UK will have been scientific and dispassionate, but its furtherance of a particular narrative appears not to be entirely impartial. Would the research have been so widely publicised if its findings had been different?

Myths are a feature of both geography and history – commonly held ideas and notions which have little basis in fact. The death of King Harold at the Battle of Hastings in 1066 is an example. Conventional wisdom has it that he died as the result of an arrow hitting him in the eye. The only evidence for this, in fact, is the depiction in the Bayeux Tapestry of an unidentified soldier, among a group of others, with an arrow in what might be his eye, near but not directly beneath a Latin caption reading 'King Harold was killed'. There is another soldier near the caption, who is more conspicuously dying and does not have an arrow in his eye. In geography, the cascades and tumbling white water that characterise the upper stages of a river suggest that this is the section of a system when water will be flowing fastest. In fact, water in the middle of a wide, later-stage river is likely to be flowing much faster because it is unaffected by friction with the bed or sides. So, what is the role of enquiry in relation to myths?

Marwick (2001) stresses the vital role that historians and their enquiries have in dispelling myths about the past, especially those that might foster prejudice. Distortions of history propounded by the South African education system during the Apartheid years or the rewriting of history in the former Soviet Union are cited as examples, as are the myths of ethnic superiority and/or persecution that have underpinned conflicts in the former Yugoslavia and Northern Ireland. He states that history 'challenges and deflates myths, while at the same time explaining their origin and significance' (Marwick, 2001: 33). He provides a diagram to represent the process of history and how the past, sources and myths are related (see Figure 2.3).

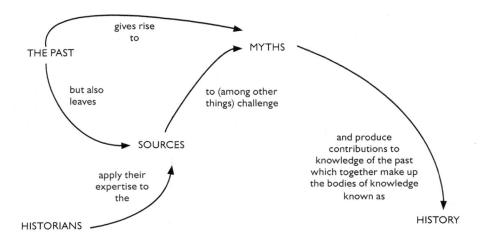

Figure 2.3   Marwick, *The New Nature of History* (2001), Palgrave Macmillan

Though myths may not be so prevalent in geography, the enquiry process can play a key role in challenging the misinformation and bias that surround contentious issues, such as migration, and catastrophes like Hurricane Katrina. Analysis of evidence often reveals that myths generated by tabloid newspaper headlines about immigration into the UK have either little substance in fact or are the product of distortion. One example is a story in the *Daily Mail* in October 2009 with the headline: 'More than 700 migrants a day have been let in to Britain'. This was based on a government-sponsored report, 'Economic Performance: A migration perspective' (Department of Communities and Local Government [DCLG], September 2009), which reported that 'recent evidence indicates that the 2001 figure of 4.3 million foreign-born people in the UK could have grown further by more than two million in the last eight years' (DCLG, 2009: 12). The speculative tone of the quotation is not conveyed by the headline and the simple arithmetic on which the headline is based is flawed – 2 million divided by 2,920 days (eight years) gives a figure of 684.9, which is less than 700, not more.

The aftermath of Hurricane Katrina in August 2005 was characterised by many conflicting news reports about the quality of flood defences in New Orleans. Some sources suggested that levees and flood walls had been built 'on the cheap' and accusations of corruption were rife. Others argued that no flood defences could have protected the 'shrunken, degraded and essentially defenceless landscape' (*The New York Times*, 5 September 2005) of the Mississippi delta from catastrophic flooding. Myths about race and political inertia were perpetuated. Analysis of the evidence suggests that the disaster that befell New Orleans was not the result of one error, but many. The levees that protected most of the city were simply overwhelmed by depths of flood water they had not been designed to cope with. Other breached defences were undermined by erosion. But environmental degradation played its part too, and human intervention in natural processes contributed to the inundation of the Louisiana coast. There was no mythical single cause.

 Exploring myths with Year 6

As part of a unit of work on Ancient Greece, a Year 6 teacher read some extracts from a children's adaptation of Homer's *Odyssey* as a serial story. He explained that the story told the tale of a Greek soldier's long and tortuous journey home after the Trojan War and, like all good stories, probably it had been exaggerated and changed in the retelling over many years. The extracts included Odysseus's outwitting of Polyphemus the Cyclops, his encounter with Circe, his temptation by the Sirens and his fight with the sea monster Scylla. After each episode the teacher asked the children to record, on a simply structured worksheet, the elements of the story which they thought might be true and which they thought were exaggerated or fantasy. Although the children thought that much of the story of the Cyclops was fantasy, they recognised that the whirlpool of Charybdis, into which Odysseus's ship was nearly dragged, might be factually based. To conclude the story, the teacher shared a map of the Odyssey (www.uwm.edu/Course/mythology/1200/2001.jpg) on an interactive whiteboard and pointed out where some of the events took place, including identifying Charybdis as representing the dangerous, swirling currents of the Straits of Messina between Sicily and Italy. The activity made the key point that an understanding of geographical features can begin to explain historical myths.

So, how do the enquiry processes in history and geography relate to enquiry-led learning?

Cooper (2000) relates Collingwood's analysis of history to children in the primary school, using the term 'historical enquiry' to describe the process of interpretation. She argues that making probabilistic inferences, supporting opinions with arguments and accepting that differing interpretations may be valid are all important skills and experiences for the intellectual growth of children. Marwick's analysis can also contribute. For children to do history, they must engage, like historians, with primary sources and begin to make deductions based on evidence, recognising strengths and limitations. Secondary sources will have a place in establishing contexts and connections, but access to historical evidence is essential. Furthermore, if they are to behave like historians, children must then communicate their newfound knowledge.

Views on young children's ability to cope with these concepts and ideas have changed over time. In the 1960s, history in primary schools usually presented children with a single perspective on the past and stereotypical representations of people and events. The Plowden Report on *Children and their primary schools* (1967) famously called for more research into children's understandings in relation to history and marvelled that 'children may study it in such detail that probing questions are asked, connections are seen and discoveries are made . . . authentically from written sources' (p. 226). The history curriculum in National Curriculum 2000, informed by the work of Donaldson (1978) and others on children's problem-solving abilities, required children to engage in making inferences and interpretations. This is not to say that there was an expectation that children would create Collingwood's 'web of imaginative construction' (1946: 242), but that they would engage with historical material in ways that equate with what historians do.

So, how does doing history relate to enquiry-led learning? In short, history is a process of enquiry, using particular methods to analyse particular types of evidence. Children cannot do history without doing enquiry. The two are inextricably linked, if not synonymous. But can the same be said of geography? Is geographical enquiry as fundamental to the subject as the process of interpretation is fundamental to history? The answer is not so clear.

If doing history implies engaging in a process, does doing geography imply something similar? For a start, the scope of geography is immense, so a single investigative process, no matter how complex, is unlikely to suffice. The *Penguin Dictionary of Geography* (1998) describes geography as

The study that deals with the material and human phenomena in the space accessible to human beings and their instruments, especially the patterns of, and variation in, their distribution in that space, on all scales, in the past and present.

(p. 166)

It then goes on to separately define physical and human geography in more detail. The issue of defining geography is, in itself, contentious. In a seminal article in Johnston's *The Future of Geography* (1985), Eliot Hurst argues that most definitions (like the one above) focus on the notion of 'space' as a the key concept in the subject. He is deeply unimpressed by this view. Geography as the study of 'space' and its use is a reification – a fallacy of treating an abstraction as if it were a real thing. Space is just one variable in the patterns that geographers observe on the earth's surface with social, political and economic variables being, at least, equally important.

Whereas history concerns itself with analysing evidence of (predominantly) human actions and motivations in the past, geography encompasses the human and the physical world in both past and present. It looks at patterns and processes evident at the tops of mountains and in the depths of the oceans; in remote, underpopulated regions and in the heart of world cities; in microclimates and in the earth's climate as a whole. It links with and subsumes other disciplines, such as geology, meteorology and sociology, and adapts their paradigms and methodologies to make sense of the world.

So, what do geographers *do*? How can children *behave* like geographers? Whereas historians generally practise their trade in the academic world and its media offshoots, a geographer could be an academic researcher, a mapmaker, a journalist, an explorer (yes, there are still places on the planet to be fully mapped and explored), an urban planner, a seismologist, a tourism or environmental manager, an hydrologist – if not quite endless, the list is extensive! They might work in education, in the business world, in government or in a non-governmental organisation, such as a charity, especially those concerned with development issues. The skills used will be hugely variable – from analysing trends and data using computer-based, geographical information systems to detailed measurement of physical processes, such as erosion, through hands-on fieldwork. All geographers, like historians, are enquirers – seeking answers to questions based on evidence – but there the similarity ends because the range of questions and the range of processes to answer them are infinitely more varied in geography.

The curriculum itself provides its own complications, in that it concerns itself with more than just teaching and learning of knowledge, understandings and skills. There are also requirements concerned with values and attitudes: children should express likes and dislikes about localities, improve their environment and consider issues of sustainability. This values-based thread of geography is not uncontentious; writing on the Campaign for Real Education website, Standish (2004) argues that it tends to 'inhibit intellectual thought, it is also anti-democratic and intrusive into the private lives of children'. He further develops his arguments in his book *Global Perspectives in the Geography Curriculum* (2008), where he contends that the concept of global citizenship has refocused geographical education away from intellectual development onto the 'values, attitudes and psychological well-being of students' (2008: 180). Given current priorities and concerns in relation to environmental degradation and climate change, it is a strand of geographical education that is unlikely to go away, however.

So, how does the process of geographical enquiry fit into this picture? A clue to the answer may lie in a quotation from Marcia Foley, Adviser for Geography with Kent Advisory Service, who writes in her advice to primary teachers on the Kent County Council website, 'The *best* process for learning geography is that of geographical enquiry' (2009). Given its breadth and scope, an enquiry approach is not the only way to learn geography, but it is the best way. It provides a way through the complexities of the subject and means by which the elements of geography – human, physical, skills, knowledge, values, attitudes – can be accessed and applied to questions, issues and problems. Enquiry-led learning reflects how geographers *do* their subject, from whatever part of the discipline they come.

 To think about

Deduction and induction

The essential differences between the process of deduction on which history is based and the more scientific process of induction, which underpins much of geography, can be illustrated most easily by a scenario.

A car driver pulls up at a T-junction. He is on a minor road, with traffic on a major road in front of him. He wants to turn left into the major road, so looks to his right to see if there is a gap in the traffic. He sees a red car approaching quite slowly, with its left indicator flashing. It would appear that the red car is going to turn into the minor road, so it is safe to drive out in front of it. If the car driver adopts an inductive approach, then he pulls out, because in all previous situations he has encountered, the flashing left indicator has indicated an intention to turn left. If he is deductive, however, he does not rely on precedents, but waits for the car to turn, as logic suggests that he can only be sure of the red car's intentions when the turn has been executed.

Usually, the inductive driver will be correct in his assumption and the deductive driver seem overcautious but, as any road user will confirm, a flashing indicator does not always indicate an intention to turn – it might have been put on in error or the red car's driver might suddenly decide that he is about to make a wrong turning and accelerate forwards. What approach, do you think, the *Highway Code* instructs in this situation? Inductive or deductive?

Unlike historical enquiry with its reliance on logical deduction from cause to effect – Collingwood's 'web of imaginative construction stretched between certain fixed points' (1946: 242) – geographical enquiry, like scientific method, is often an inductive process. It describes and predicts behaviours, patterns and processes based on previous precedents, rather than logical deductions. In studying the process of globalisation, for example, a human geographer can predict that multinational companies will tend to move mass production of goods to low-waged economies. This is based on many previous precedents and describes a strong likelihood, rather than a certainty – a multinational may for some reason decide to counter the trend and site a factory in a relatively high-waged location. Similarly, in physical geography, patterns and processes in river systems can be predicted based on a multitude of observations and measurements of systems in a range of landscapes and environments. In history, it may not be possible to find numerous precedents on which to build inductive reasoning, so logical deduction takes its place. Of course, there will be exceptions in both subjects – a geographer might deduce the origin of an uncharacteristic rock in a glacial valley by charting the path of the glacier that carried it or a historian might use precedents to interpret the significance of a political speech. Deduction and induction are characteristic features of the subjects, however, and provide underpinning processes on which historical and geographical enquiries are built.

Summary

In conclusion, the distinctive elements of the enquiry processes in history and geography can be summarised, as shown in Table 2.1.

Table 2.1 Elements of the enquiry processes in history and geography

	History	Geography
Enquiry	Fundamental	Necessary, but not essential
Skills	Interpretation Interpolation	Varied and drawn from a range of disciplines
Reasoning	Deductive and logical	Inductive and scientific
Imagination	Essential to interpretation	Useful for visualisation and prediction
Sources	Clear dichotomy of primary and secondary	No clear dichotomy of primary and secondary

How some of these elements can be translated into learning activities is explored in Chapter 5. Of course, it would be unrealistic and unreasonable to expect children to grapple with all of these elements in Foundation Stage or Y1, so a progressive introduction to the complexities of enquiry will be fundamental to primary history and geography. Issues and perspectives on progression are explored in Chapter 6.

References

Carr, E.H. (1961) *What is History?* Harmondsworth: Penguin.

Central Advisory Council for Education (England) (1967) *Children and their primary schools* (Plowden Report). London: HMSO.

Clark, A. (1998) *The Penguin Dictionary of Geography*. London: Penguin Books.

Collingwood, R.G. (1946) *The Idea of History*. Oxford: Oxford University Press.

Cooper, H. (2000) *The Teaching of History in Primary Schools*, 3rd edn. London: David Fulton.

DairyNZ (2010) *DairyNZ Corporate Brochure*. Available at: www.milksmart.co.nz/DownloadResource.aspx?id=611

Department for Communities and Local Government (DCLG) (2009) *Regional Economic Performance – A Migration Perspective: Economics Paper 4*. Available at: www.communities.gov.uk/publications/communities/ecoperformancemigration4

Donaldson, M. (1978) *Children's Minds*. London: Fontana.

Draw-a-Scientist Test (22 October 2011) In *Wikipedia, The Free Encyclopedia*. Retrieved from http://en.wikipedia.org/w/index.php?title=Draw-a-Scientist_Test&oldid=456852534

Foley, M. (2009) *What is Geographical Enquiry?* Available at: www.kenttrustweb.org.uk/kentict/kentict_subjects_geo_enq_intro.cfm

Johnston, R.J. (ed.) (1985) *The Future of Geography*. Cambridge: Cambridge University Press.

Marwick, A. (2001) *The New Nature of History*. Basingstoke: Palgrave.

Mink, L. (1968) 'Collingwood's Dialectic of History', in *History and Theory*, 7 (February): 3–37.

New York Times (2005) 'Redemption in the Bayou', 5 September. Available at: www.nytimes.com/2005/09/05/opinion/05mon3.html

Standish, A. (2004) Geography's New Agenda. Available from the Campaign for Real Education website: www.cre.org.uk/docs/geography.html

Standish, A. (2008) *Global Perspectives in the Geography Curriculum*. London: Routledge.

Starkey, D. (2005) 'What history should we be teaching in Britain in the 21st century?' Paper presented at the Institute of Historical Research History in British Education Conference, February, University of London.

Symington, D. and Spurling, H. (1990) 'The "Draw a Scientist Test": interpreting the data', in *Research in Science and Technological Education*, 8(1): 75–7.

CHAPTER 3

ENQUIRY OUTSIDE THE CLASSROOM

By the end of this chapter you will be able to:

- explain the importance of learning outside the classroom (fieldwork) to the enquiry process in the humanities;
- describe the benefits and limitations of different places where learning outside the classroom (fieldwork) may take place;
- describe the implications for teaching and learning of historical and geographical enquiry through different types of learning outside the classroom (fieldwork).

Geography is all around us and is a practical subject about the real world in which children live and work. It is a subject of relevance to life in the twenty-first century, both now and for the future. History provides us with a context from which to understand ourselves and others, and helps us understand how the world works. Knowledge of the past is required for understanding present realities and future possibilities.

Most of us, or all of us, begin to learn Geography as soon as we can walk, if not sooner, and we are studying it more or less all our lives. It is true that we can do this to a large extent unconsciously, for we cannot take even the shortest walk and find our way home again, nor look at the hills and valleys, the roads and rivers of the countryside, nor at the streets and buildings, the tram lines and railway stations of the town, without learning geography.

(A.J. Herbertson, 1898, cited in Catlin, 1993)

Children are extremely curious and should be given the opportunity to explore and to make sense of the world around them by studying outside the classroom, making links between feelings and learning. What they see, hear, taste, touch, smell, do, feel, imagine and sense provide avenues to deep and meaningful learning. OFSTED, in their *Learning Outside the Classroom Manifesto* (2006), stated that

The first-hand experiences of learning outside the classroom can help to make subjects more vivid and interesting for children and enhance their understanding. It can also contribute significantly to children's personal, social and emotional development.

(DfES, 2006: 4)

A lot of what happens in the classroom masquerades as learning, but many activities fail to engage or stimulate the children, because they simply focus on the memorisation and neat recording of facts and information at the expense of understanding and learning. Learning outside the classroom can motivate the children in their learning; learning outside the classroom through enquiry fully engages and challenges the children, ensuring real learning takes place and so maximising achievement.

Fieldwork: learning outside the classroom in humanities

Learning outside the classroom in primary history and geography is usually referred to as fieldwork, the 'field' being the place where the learning is taking place and 'fieldwork' the activities undertaken. The 'field of study' may be the local area or further afield, a historical building or a museum. The field is the key source of primary geographical and historical data and information. Fieldwork bridges the classroom and the real world, helping to transfer learning experienced outside to the classroom and vice versa. The very best learning in both geography and in history occurs through first-hand experience, when children are active learners, engaged in the process of enquiry, posing and answering questions.

> Tell me and I will forget;
> Show me and I may remember;
> Involve me and I will understand.
> (Chinese Proverb attributed to Xun Zi,
> a Confucian philosopher)

Fieldwork promotes the development of a wide range of skills, many of which are transferable. These can include enquiry and investigative skills such as observational skills, data collection and recording, data analysis and interpretation, and making generalisations from the evidence. Fieldwork also contributes to children's personal and social development, as it involves children interacting and communicating with each other, collaborating, listening to the views and suggestions of others and working as a team. It helps children develop an understanding of themselves, reflecting on and making sense of their own views about the world, such as environmental issues or what happened in the past, and on what influences their decisions. Fieldwork develops an understanding that other children may have different views and opinions, so contributing to the development of empathy with others. It also provides opportunity for children to appreciate and explore their emotional responses to a wide range of environments, buildings, artefacts and artwork.

> Learning outside the classroom is about raising achievement . . . in which direct experience is of prime importance. This is not only about **what** we learn but importantly **how** and **where** we learn.
> (DfES, 2006: 3)

Enquiry through fieldwork and first-hand experience provides opportunity for learning about the present, the past and the possible impact of actions on the future, in both the natural and man-made world. It is the process through which children actively learn about the world, making sense of it for themselves. By appealing to different learning styles and taking account of the multisensory methodology of fieldwork, enquiry through fieldwork has the potential to develop good, effective learning. Children thrive and achieve and their learning is maximised.

David Bell, former HM Chief Inspector of Schools, said:

Geography enables us to understand change, conflict and the key issues which impact on our lives today and will affect our futures tomorrow.

(Bell, 2004)

Fieldwork probably results in the most exciting and memorable learning experiences in the lives of many children. Memories of these experiences usually remain with us all through our lifetime.

Learning outside the classroom – but where and why?

Well planned fieldwork in geography adds clear value to learning in the subject as well as providing a positive contribution to the wider curriculum.

(OFSTED, 2008: 33)

Learning outside the classroom, including fieldwork in geography and history, can take place in a variety of locations and over different lengths of time. It can be undertaken in the Early Years setting, or at school, the school grounds/school site, the local area, or places further afield such as a contrasting locality, a visit to a museum, historic building or heritage site, and may last for a few minutes, a day, or take the form of a residential visit lasting a number of days (Table 3.1). The DfEE and QCA, in *The National Curriculum, Handbook for primary teachers in England*, 1999, stated that fieldwork has the potential to provide experiential opportunities 'to enable pupils to respond positively to opportunities, challenges and responsibilities, to manage risk and to cope with change and adversity' (DfEE and QCA, 1999: 12).

Table 3.1 The advantages to enquiry in humanities of 'learning outside' the classroom, using different sites and for different lengths of time

Location	Advantages
School building	• The investigations are relevant to *all* children participating in the enquiry.
	The school building offers
	• first-hand experiences for children; • a safe location for children to work in; • accessibility at no cost (no transport costs or entry charges); • opportunity to visit frequently to observe changes over time.

Table 3.1 continues overleaf

Location	Advantages
School grounds/school site	• The school grounds (outdoor classroom) are the most accessible fieldwork site. • The investigations are relevant to *all* children participating in the enquiry. Education Minister Stephen Twigg MP said, at the National School Grounds Week launch 2003, that school grounds offer 'uniquely rich and rewarding learning experiences for children of all ages, backgrounds and abilities, giving them a greater understanding of the world around them'. 'Quality learning experiences in "real" situations have the capacity to raise achievement across a range of subjects and to develop better personal and social skills'. (DFES, 2006: 3) The school grounds/school site offers • first-hand experiences for children; • a safe location for children to work in; • easy access to opportunities for children to learn outside the classroom; • accessibility at no cost (no transport costs or entry charges); • opportunity to visit frequently to observe changes over time.
Local area	• The area in the immediate locality of the school provides a rich, versatile learning resource, in which learners can develop the skills to explore their local environment. • The investigations are relevant to *all* children participating in the enquiry. The local area offers • first-hand experiences for children; • easy access to opportunities for children to learn outside the classroom; • accessibility at no cost, wealth of opportunities usually within walking distance (no transport costs or entry charges); • opportunity to visit frequently to observe changes over time.
Places further afield – day/half-day visit	• Moving away from the children's familiar environment can provide new outlooks, more distant and challenging environments and a sharing of new experiences. • A sense of adventure, a different and engaging experience shared with peers, ownership of the experiences can provide a focal point for learning and exploring. Places further afield – day/half-day visit – offers • first-hand experiences of more distant and challenging environments (rural or urban), environmental issues, processes; visits to museum and art galleries; • enriching and broadening experiences that complement and reinforce 'classroom' learning; • opportunities to develop and use different ways of learning; • opportunities of working co-operatively and developing an understanding of the roles and contributions of others.

Location	• Advantage
Places further afield – residential visits	• Residential experiences enable children to develop key life skills, building confidence, self-esteem, communication and team working. These experiences help equip children with skills applicable and transferable to everyday life. • Children are able to share new experiences with peers.
	Places further afield – a residential visit/experience – offers
	• first-hand experiences of more distant and challenging environments (rural or urban), environmental issues, processes, visits to outdoor centres, museums and art galleries; • enriching and broadening experiences that complement and reinforce 'classroom' learning; • opportunities to develop and use different ways of learning; • opportunities of working co-operatively and developing an understanding of the roles and contributions of others; • opportunity for children to explore and realise their own potential; to recognise success for themselves and others; to value themselves and others.

Geography fieldwork using the school and school grounds

Many different enquiries can take place at the different sites and over different lengths of time.

A sample of overarching geographical enquiry questions and activities for using the school building includes the following.

- How accessible is our school for a blind person? A wheelchair user?
- Can we organise the school office to be easier for the bursar and secretary to use?
- How can we reorganise our classroom? Consider how the room is to be used. Measure, draw to scale, etc. Decide what furniture and resources to include and where to site them. Present to the class, giving reasons for choices made.
- How much water/food do we waste?
- How much energy do we use?
- What happens to all the waste we produce?

A sample of overarching geographical enquiry questions and activities for using the school grounds includes the following.

- How do we really get to know our school grounds?

Try this activity

A sample of activities using the school grounds as part of enquiries includes the following.

- Using digital photos of features located in the school grounds, taken from unusual angles or very close up, and a map, ask the children to find the locations of the features and mark them on the map.

- Ask children to create their own trails using photographs taken from unusual angles.

- Ask children to stand still and close their eyes. What can they hear, smell, touch, taste? Ask them to open their eyes – what can they see? Record their experiences.

- A fieldwork starter activity for all key stages, which gets children really thinking about their environment and surroundings, is 'I am a camera' activity. Ask children to work in pairs. One child closes their eyes or puts on a blindfold while the other child guides them to a particular viewpoint. The sighted child then describes the view in detail to their partner, as if they were a camera, taking a photo. Ask the unsighted child to remove the blindfold/open their eyes and compare.

- Children consider the source and type of sounds they can hear and produce soundscapes. In pairs, one child closes their eyes and names every sound they can hear over a period of time. The other child records for the unsighted child. Children open eyes and discuss. What do these sounds tell children about the place they are investigating? Ask if sounds fall into any categories, e.g. human or natural. From the centre of a piece of paper, ask each child to draw a line in the direction of each sound they hear. Ask children to indicate volume by the thickness of the line. Can they spot any other patterns?

- Ask the children to compile an 'emotion map' of the school grounds or a particular route. This activity offers a good opportunity to talk about similarities and differences and our own uniqueness and to build relationships through sharing personal responses to place.

  Which areas felt safe?
  Which ones felt frightening?
  Did everyone feel the same? If not, why not?
  What do other children/adults think about these spaces and how could we find out?

- Investigate what happens to water on different surfaces and slopes. Where does the water go?

- How can we improve the school grounds? Can we help develop an area of the school grounds (e.g. for wildlife, as a quiet area, as a garden)? Which area? How big? What's going in it? How much will it cost? How long will it take? Draw a scale plan. Write a list of jobs and prioritise.

- How can we improve playground markings? Measure the playground. Investigate markings. Design some markings. What do children want? Conduct a survey. Produce a scheme for remarking the playground. Make a scale drawing. Does it all fit? How much will it all cost?

History fieldwork using the local area

A sample of overarching historical enquiry questions and activities for using the local area include the following.

- How has this placed changed? Use old photographs of the local area, e.g. 1880s, 1930s, 1960s, 1980s. Fieldwork: children stand where the photograph(s) were taken and record changes – look carefully at buildings, road, the way people are dressed, cars, etc.

- Change of use of building, for example, old mill or warehouses on canalside. Children to devise enquiry questions, for example, what was this building used for in the past? How has the use changed? Why? What is the building being used for now? (Possibly luxury apartments/museums/retail centre, etc.)

- How has this farm changed over the past 50 years? Field visit to farm and interviews with farmer/farm manager. Focus on mechanisation and diversification, for example, barn conversions, offering B&B, etc.

What are the educational benefits of fieldwork?

Fieldwork and learning outside the classroom is not an end in itself, but it provides the opportunity and context in which children can undertake their enquiries and practise their investigative skills. It also helps them build bridges between theory and the real world.

OFSTED, in *Geography in schools: changing practice*, stated:

Follow up from fieldwork also provides very good support for extended writing, numeracy linked to the analysis of data, sketching, map work, formulating hypotheses and thinking skills.

(OFSTED, 2008: 34)

Quality learning experiences in 'real' situations have the capacity to raise academic achievement across a range of subjects. The benefits of fieldwork are discussed in the following 'To think about' and are based on the *Learning Outside the Classroom Manifesto* and the National Curriculum.

 To think about

With a partner, discuss the merits and advantages of using the outdoors to support learning through enquiry in the humanities. Also consider any disadvantages or issues.

The list below, compiled from the *Learning Outside the Classroom Manifesto* (p.4) and the 1999 National Curriculum handbook for teachers, suggests that, when these experiences are well planned, safely managed and personalised to meet the needs of every child, they can have wide-reaching positive impacts. Discuss your views with your partner.

Learning outside the classroom can:

- stimulate, inspire and improve motivation, making learning more engaging and relevant to the children;
- develop skills and independence in a broadening range of environments;
- improve observation skills and understanding of the processes that contributed to the development of environmental features;
- provide opportunities to learn through direct, concrete experiences, enhancing the understanding that comes from observing 'real world' evidence of abstract geographical and historical concepts and processes;
- increase geographical and historical interest through interacting with the environment, thus developing active citizens and stewards of the environment;
- support the development and application of analytical skills, many of which are not used in the classroom;

- develop investigative and communicative skills and the ability to deal with uncertainty, through experiencing real-life research;
- nurture creativity;
- provide challenge and the opportunity to take acceptable levels of risk;
- improve young people's attitudes to learning;
- support the development of teamwork skills, through working co-operatively with others in a setting outside the classroom;
- support skill development, such as observation, synthesis, evaluation, reasoning, measuring skills, practical problem solving, adaptability to new demands that call upon creative solutions, etc.;
- support the use and application of new technology, e.g. use xxx to investigate and record problems and issues;
- support the development of key skills, such as communication, application of number, information technology, working with others, improving own learning performance and problem solving.

Forest Schools

A number of schools in the UK are becoming Forest Schools. The concept of Forest Schools originates in Scandinavia, where there has been a long tradition of encouraging children to play and learn outdoors. Forest Schools aim to encourage and inspire children through positive outdoor experiences. Through Forest School activities, children are helped to understand the natural environment and develop an appreciation of their surroundings. They grow up caring for their environment, which develops a sense of responsibility towards it and provides the foundations of sustainability.

Through their own enquiries and child-initiated activities, children learn about the natural environment, how to handle risks, use their own initiative to solve problems and to co-operate with others. Forest Schools offer children time to thoroughly explore their thoughts and feelings. This time and reflective practice helps children to develop an understanding of the world, the environment and everything within it through the use of emotions, imagination and senses. This supports enquiry in the humanities, particularly geography, as it gives the children the opportunity and time to develop their enquiries.

Types of fieldwork

In the primary school, there are basically three common approaches to learning outside the classroom in geography and history. There is the 'look and see' visit, the teacher-centred and expository (field teaching) and the more investigative, enquiry-based and pupil-centred (enquiry-based fieldwork). The approach depends on the nature and objectives of the lesson.

(i) Look and see

This is often seen as the traditional approach to teaching and learning outside the classroom. The teacher is the provider of all information, while the children are passive receivers. An example of the 'look and see' approach' is a visit to the Roman walls and amphitheatre in Chester, where the teacher walks the children around, telling them about various aspects of Roman Chester. This approach may involve children in the observation and description of a scene or a building.

(ii) Field teaching

Field teaching engages the children as more active learners. It supports children in developing and practising fieldwork techniques, at the direction of the teacher. It involves children making careful observations, using maps, artefacts and/or historical records, using different measuring equipment depending on the focus, recording data and measurements and making notes. It helps give the children confidence in their skills and ability to solve problems and is an integral part of the learning experience. However, very little opportunity exists for children's own lines of investigation, questioning or enquiry. This approach may involve children in suggesting possible explanations based on the data they collect.

An example of field teaching or teacher-directed fieldwork is investigating the weather in the school grounds. The focus is on learning how to use the measuring equipment to measure different elements of weather such as temperature, wind and rainfall. Through this fieldwork, illustrated in Table 3.2, the children may learn to use a thermometer, a maximum and minimum thermometer, a rain gauge, an anemometer (to measure wind speed) and a wind vane (to determine wind direction).

Table 3.2   Practising and developing fieldwork skills and techniques through expository and teacher-centred fieldwork

What is this place like? – Microclimates: weather in the school grounds

Counting, measuring, collecting and recording

Temperature	Using a large, easy-to-read thermometer, children can record temperature using the Celsius scale (degrees Celsius – °C).
	• Each day, at the same time, measure the temperature at one set site. Look at the range and temperature pattern over a set period of time.
	• On each day, measure the temperature at set sites around the school grounds at 9 a.m., 11 a.m., 1 p.m. and 3 p.m. Find the average temperature for each site for each day.
	• Use a maximum and minimum thermometer. Record temperature daily at a set time. Look at the daily range in temperature.
Rainfall	Using non-standard measures
	• children can draw round the circumference of a puddle and, after a set amount of time, return to draw and measure again. Is there any difference? Return again. Is there any difference?
	Using a rain gauge, children can record the rainfall in centimetres/ millimetres.
	• Once a day, measure the rainfall at each of the set sites around the school where the temperature is being recorded.
Wind strength	Using non-standard measures
	• children can measure the strength of the wind using non-standard units using materials of varying thickness secured on a stick.
	Using an anemometer
	• children can measure the strength of the wind in kilometres per hour. Measure the wind speed at each of the set sites around the school where the temperature is being recorded.
	Using a wind vane
	• children can identify the direction of the wind.
Cloud cover	Children can measure the amount of cloud cover.
	• Using a ten-by-ten grid at a window, count the number of squares covered by cloud. This will give you the percentage cover.

Presenting and summarising (tables, charts and graphs)

Temperature	• Children draw charts and graphs for the temperature recordings at one site or at different sites and at different times.
Rainfall	• Children construct tables and graphs for daily readings at different sites.

Table 3.2 continues overleaf

Interpreting, analysing and predicting (making sense of data)	
Temperature	Which area around school is the warmest? Why? Where would you site a picnic bench? When was the coldest/hottest day/night? During which months would you advise your dad to leave his car in the garage?
Rainfall	What happens to a puddle over time? Where does the water go? If it was a sunny and windy day, would the puddle go more quickly? During which months was rainfall heavy/light? Above/below average rainfall? In which month is it most likely that there will be a hosepipe ban? In which month would you advise the head teacher to hold Sports Day?
Wind strength	Which areas around school are windiest and why? Where would you fly a kite? Where is the best place to have a barbecue? Where would you site a wind vane? Where would you hang your clothes to dry?

In history, an example of teacher-directed fieldwork may involve a visit to a museum, where children are taught the skill of how to 'read' an artefact. It is explained to the children that history, the story of the past, is often told through objects or artefacts made or used by people in those times. Children look at and handle an object (the artefact) and describe the artefact's physical characteristics. They may then be taught to ask five questions to ask about any object:

- What is it?
- What was it used for?
- Who made the object? Who used it? Who owned it?
- What is the object's social significance?
- How has it changed over time? Do we use the same object today? If we no longer use the object, what has taken its place?

(iii) Enquiry-based fieldwork

Enquiry-based fieldwork sharpens and deepens learners' understanding of geography and the progressive development of geographical skills.

(Ofsted, 2008: 34)

Enquiry-based fieldwork is a framework for learning which involves a large degree of pupil ownership and enables children to structure their own learning. Initially the children are supported by the teacher in devising an overarching enquiry question as the focus for the fieldwork, a question that is interesting, hooks the children into the learning and gets them talking and thinking straight away. The teacher is aware of how the fieldwork enquiry fits into the planning for the unit of work. For example, in history, when modelling the constructing of enquiry questions relating to a fieldwork visit to a historical building, the teacher will consider which of the range of historical concepts the enquiry should focus on. Gradually, the children take more responsibility for their learning, and become more involved in devising the initial and subsidiary enquiry questions, in planning and then carrying out the investigations in the field.

With a problem-solving focus, enquiry-based fieldwork can take either an inductive or deductive approach to learning. In the inductive approach, the fieldwork will start with an observation of a phenomenon, which raises questions and subsequently shapes the investigation. In the deductive approach to fieldwork, the enquiry begins with a hypothesis and, through fieldwork, the hypothesis is either confirmed or contradicted.

Examples of enquiry-based fieldwork

Two examples of enquiry-based fieldwork in geography and two in history are illustrated below. The first of the examples in geography is a case study based on a proposal to develop an area of woodland (a); and the second an activity to try focusing on coastal erosion (b). The first of the two enquiries in history is a suggested activity/visit to a Victorian classroom to support children in their enquiry to find out about what life was like in Victorian times (c); and the second a case study based on a field visit to find out what it was like to live during the Second World War (d).

Enquiry-based fieldwork: geography examples

(a) Should developers be allowed to build a holiday village in the forest?

Children at a local primary school decided to investigate and find out more information about plans to build a holiday village of log cabins, a new visitors' centre, a restaurant, a concert venue and shops in part of a local forest. They wanted to investigate how the local area would change and to find out about the impact, both positive and negative, that this development could have on the local area and on local people and current users of the forest.

The enquiry questions proposed by children were:

- Who owns the forest?
- How many people visit the forest currently?
- How much of the forest would be taken up by the planned village?
- Who can we talk to to get the facts?
- Who would be affected and how? Who would benefit? Why? Who would not benefit? Why?
- Who uses the forest now? What activities take place?
- What impact will there be on the wildlife, the trees, etc. What about the protected toads? What about the area of forest which is a SSSI (Site of Special Scientific Interest)?
- How congested would the small roads be? Would there be sufficient parking?
- Can a forest of this size sustain the increase in visitors?

Activities undertaken by the children included field visit(s) to the forest and classroom research, preparation and follow-up.

Fieldwork and in-class research: activities to find out about the trees, plants, animals and birds that live in the forest.

In-class research: the children knew that the forest has several Sites of Special Scientific Interest (SSSI). Half the class undertook various research activities to find out: what SSSI sites are; which plants or animals in the forest were endangered and/or protected; how this development might impact on them.

The other half of the class found out what attractions and activities were already present in the forest (e.g. walking, wheelchair-accessible trails, cycling, learning programmes for schools, orienteering, high ropes trail – a treetop adventure course of rope bridges – live music in the forest, etc.)

Fieldwork and in-class preparation: who uses the forest and what for? In class, the children prepared questionnaires and then conducted interviews in the field (i.e. in the forest). The children interviewed people who use the forest, such as walkers, cyclists, horse riders, birdwatchers; local people; people who work in the forest, cafe/restaurant owners, etc., the widest cross-section possible.

Fieldwork and in-class preparation: how do local people feel about the proposed development? In class, the children prepared questions to ask local people. They then interviewed a Forest Ranger; log cabin development proposer; member of badger protection league; local councillor; local MP; cafe owner; local farmer; police; local planner; organiser of music in the forest, headteacher of local school, etc.

In-class follow-up: from the evidence they had collected, the children, in groups, listed reasons why a new holiday village would be good and reasons why it would be bad. They discussed who the new holiday village would help and who it would not help? As a whole class, they listened to everyone's points of view. They then held a debate in class.

In-class follow-up: The children wrote a letter to the local council giving reasons why they felt the holiday village should/should not be allowed to be built (discussion/persuasion genre).

Members from the planning department of the local council and the local MP visited the school, to listen to the children's viewpoints.

 Try this activity

(b) Why is this coast wearing away? (Coastal erosion)

Activities, focusing on coastal erosion, to try with either Year 5 or Year 6 children on a field visit to the coast, including classroom research, preparation and follow-up.

Fieldwork: visit a coastal area.

Fieldwork: look at the different evidence of coastal erosion. Mark these areas on a map.

Fieldwork: look for evidence of how the area has been protected in the past. Mark these on the map.

In-class research: find out about the different methods of protecting coastal areas. What might happen if the coastal area isn't protected? Who would this affect?

In-class follow-up. Ask the children, in groups, to put forward a case for one of the following:
(a)   letting an area of coast erode away naturally and for the local council not to waste any more money on protecting it;
(b)   building groynes and gabions;
(c)   building a sea wall all the way along the beach.

Hold a class debate.

Enquiry-based fieldwork: history examples

Visits to museums can be fitted in at different stages of the enquiry process and help children to build up knowledge and understanding of a historical topic or period. A visit to a museum may be used at the very beginning of the process to stimulate questions and create initial hypotheses. Then, on return to the classroom, other resources can be used to test and develop those hypotheses and build fuller answers to the questions.

 Try this activity

(c) What was it like to go to school in Victorian times?

There is no better experience for children than a visit to a Victorian schoolroom, as part of a study of what life was like in Victorian times. There are a number of Victorian schoolrooms throughout the country, where children can take part, through role-play, in a Victorian lesson, receiving 'instruction' from a stern, intimidating Victorian teacher. The smells, sights and sounds immerse the children in history and enhance the experience. The thwack of the cane, the scratchy slates, the leaky ink pens and rhythmic chanting, the straight-backed desks and the small, hard, uncomfortable seats give the children a sensual experience they will never forget! The lesson may involve handwriting practice using slates and slate pencils; arithmetic using pounds, shillings and pence; recitation and drill. In addition to taking part in Victorian lessons, there are many opportunities for children to use their historical enquiry and observational drawing skills to investigate artefacts, including logbooks from Victorian schools.

Children might develop, in the classroom, hypotheses in answer to an enquiry question. Then a visit to a museum can be used to see if their answers stand up against the evidence they see. For example, children may be exploring the story of everyday life of children during the Second World War. Examples of enquiry questions are: 'What was it like to live in a big city, such as Liverpool, Leeds or London, during the war?' 'How did people feel after hearing the declaration of war on the wireless?' 'How do you think children felt when they were evacuated to the country, leaving their parents behind?' The children may make notes and write descriptions and develop hypotheses in the classroom, based on research, using books, photographs, artefacts, internet, video and other sources. This could be followed up by a visit to a museum, such as a visit to Eden Camp, Malton, Yorkshire.

(d) What was life like for children during the Second World War?

A class of Year 5 children from a primary school in Warrington visited Eden Camp, as part of a residential visit to Yorkshire. This is what the teacher said about the experience: 'At Eden Camp, the children became aware of the reality of the war and the enormous impact it had on everyday life for people living in Britain. The displays, exhibitions and clever recreations of wartime events graphically tell the story of "The People's War", the social history of life in Britain from 1939 to 1945. By having all their senses – sight, hearing, smell and touch – stimulated through realistic tableaux, with moving figures, authentic sounds and smells, the children feel that they have been "transported back" in time to the war years. The children experience what it was like to be bombed during the Blitz; to dig an escape tunnel for the Great Escape; to feel the terror of submariners about to be torpedoed; and they can see the meagre rations each person was allowed. The visit was a vital part of our unit of work on Britain during World War II and the memories of the visit will stay with the children throughout their lives.'

However, a visit to a museum or historical site must not be a one-off 'trip', but needs to be embedded in medium-term planning and be part of a sequence of activities and learning. The class teacher must work closely with museum staff, so that the activities at the museum are closely linked to the children's questions and hypotheses. Visits to museums and/or historical sites also provide opportunities to demonstrate the transferability of the enquiry process, away from the classroom to the field.

 **Summary**

Fieldwork or learning outside the classroom is an important part of learning and teaching both in history and geography in the primary school. Taking part in fieldwork helps children understand issues which have had in the past, are having now in the present, or may have in the future, an effect on the world and people's lives. Fieldwork offers an opportunity to practise skills of observation, investigation, data collection and analysis. What the children see, hear, taste, touch, smell, do, feel and imagine helps maximise learning. Fieldwork can be inspiring and stimulating and accessible to all children, whatever their age, ability or background. It provides some of the most exciting and memorable learning experiences that children will encounter during their education.

In the primary school, there are basically three common approaches to learning outside the classroom in geography and history. There is the 'look and see' visit, the teacher-centred and expository (field teaching) approach and the more investigative, enquiry-based and pupil-centred (enquiry-based fieldwork) approach.

Fieldwork offers a rich resource for enquiry in both history and geography. Enquiry-based fieldwork is fully participatory with the children actively involved in all stages. Initially the children are supported in developing the enquiry question and subsidiary questions and also in acquiring and developing the necessary investigative skills, but gradually they take more and more ownership of the planning and become more independent learners. The range of experiences in enquiry-based fieldwork deepens and enriches subject learning, provides depth to the curriculum and also helps develop key life skills.

References

Bell, D. (2004) BBC Press Releases, 24 November.

Catlin, S. (1993) 'The Whole World in our Hands', *Geography*, 78(4): 344. The Geographical Association.

DfEE and QCA (1999) *The National Curriculum. Handbook for primary teachers in England.* London: Department for Education and Employment and Qualifications and Curriculum Authority.

DfES (2006) *Learning Outside the Classroom Manifesto.* Nottingham: DfES.

Martin, F. (2006) *Teaching Geography in Primary Schools. Learning to Live in the World.* Cambridge: Chris Kington Publishing.

OFSTED (2008) *Geography in schools: changing practice.* London: OFSTED.

Primary Geographer (Spring 2010) 'The value and importance of geography'. Sheffield: Geographical Association.

Scoffham, S. (2010) *Primary Geography (Revised) Handbook.* Sheffield: Geographical Association.

 **Websites**

Forest Schools. Further information and more details about the Forest Schools philosophy can be found at www.forestschools.com/

CHAPTER 4

RESOURCES FOR ENQUIRY

By the end of this chapter you will be able to:

- identify opportunities and contexts for using sources and resources in historical and/or geographical enquiries;
- describe the strengths of specific sources and resources for enquiries in primary history and geography;
- describe the limitations of specific sources and resources for enquiries in primary history and geography.

As discussed in Chapter 2, sources of different kinds are the fundamental subject matter of historical enquiries and provide the focus around which most geographical enquiries will be pursued. The purpose of this chapter is to outline the strengths and limitations of the main groups of sources in the context of teaching and learning, as well as indicating where some may be obtained. Their deployment and use in specific enquiries is discussed in Chapters 5 and 8.

As already mentioned in Chapter 2, the nature of primary and secondary sources has been a long-established subject of debate among academic historians. For our purposes, however, the dichotomy is simple – primary sources are those generated in the period being studied and secondary sources are the work of modern historians. Confusion between the two sometimes occurs because primary sources, such as images, may be inserted into books and websites, which are secondary sources. A primary source remains primary, even if presented by a secondary source, providing it retains its integrity as a piece of unaltered, original material. The status of sources only becomes problematic where alteration has taken place. Simplifying a written document from the past for a young audience can create issues and problems, but the document will remain a primary source if it continues to give reliable and accurate access to the views, perspectives and attitudes of the original author.

 To think about

Simplifying written sources

Below is an extract from the diary of Samuel Pepys, which describes events during the Great Fire of London in 1666.

> To St Paul's; and there walked along Watling Street, as well as I could, every creature coming away laden with goods to save and, here and there, sick people carried away in beds. Extraordinary goods carried in carts and on backs. At last met my Lord Mayor in Cannon Street, like a man spent, with a handkerchief about his neck. To the King's message he cried, like a fainting woman, 'Lord, what can I do? I am spent: people will not obey me. I have been pulling down houses, but the fire overtakes us faster than we can do it.' . . . So he left me, and I him, and walked home.

How would you simplify this passage to make it accessible for Year 2 children as a shared text, yet retain its integrity as a primary source? For an example of simplification that succeeds in retaining a good sense of the language and perspective of Pepys's diary, look at the Nuffield Primary History resources on the Great Fire on the Historical Association website: go to *Primary > Resources > Lessons and Exemplars > Lessons – Key Stage 1 > Samuel Pepys and the Great Fire of London (KS1)* and look at *Pepys and the Great Fire of London Resource A*.

Accessing and obtaining sources and resources

Two national networks in the UK are key providers of sources for history and geography, respectively. For **primary historical sources**, local authority archives and record offices provide access to a wide range of locality-based sources, including images, maps, census returns, school records and sources relating to specific local sites, such as workhouses or prisons. Archives are obviously key resources for enquiries into local history, but can also provide materials for looking at the local impact of wider historical developments, particularly changes in social conditions during the nineteenth century, a period that provides stark contrasts with the present day and a wealth of documented evidence. Every local authority has one, although they may relate to historical counties, rather than current unitary local authorities and be run by shared services. Many record offices have staff with an education-related brief, who will have experience in providing sources for schools. To access your local record office, take a look in your local phone book for archive or record office services run by your local council or search on the council's website. Many record offices and archives have made some of their sources available online, particularly images. Most charge for high-quality downloads or prints, but online access may be a useful alternative, if your local record office has limited opening hours or is geographically distant.

 Website

The ARCHON directory on the National Archives website provides a searchable database of local archives, which includes private repositories of sources, as well as local authority record offices. Each entry gives address, contact details and web links as well as an indication of the sources that are held – www.nationalarchives. gov.uk/archon

The other network which can provide material for enquiries is the network of Development Education Centres (DECs) across the UK. Founded to promote awareness of international development issues, most DECs are resource centres, which sell and/or loan materials, such as teaching packs and boxes of artefacts, related to developing countries. They are an obvious **source of materials for geographical enquiries** about contrasting localities and related issues, but can also provide sources for exploration of historical themes, such as colonialism and slavery.

Website

To find your local DEC, go to the 'Our Network' section of the Think Global website, the national association to which all Development Education Centres belong: www.think-global.org.uk

Introducing Tutankhamun's Tomb

A teacher of a Year 2 class decided, for a unit on famous people, to focus on Tutankhamun. Taking into account the interests of the children in her class, she decided to begin by looking at the discovery of his tomb by Howard Carter in 1922. This provided a starting point which would allow for many opportunities to include the life and culture of Ancient Egypt in a variety of lessons.

To begin this unit of work, the teacher devised an introductory activity which would spark children's interest and curiosity by using **objects and sources** in the form of a treasure trail. This involved the teaching assistant bringing in a 'missing backpack' and asking if it belonged to anyone. When no one claimed it, the teacher looked inside and, rather theatrically, produced items that might be associated with an explorer, including binoculars, a sun hat, magnifying glass and a map. The map showed the children a route around the playground and, as they followed it as a class, different clues were discovered, such as bandages, jewellery and a piece of papyrus. These were then taken back to the classroom where the children were able to question and explore their finds in groups and as a class. After listening to some ideas, the teacher then put an image of Howard Carter on the interactive whiteboard and the children talked about who he might be. Some said he was a scientist and others said he looked like an explorer. The teacher then shared with the children who he was and how he had followed a trail in a distant land called Egypt, similar to the one followed by the class, to find the tomb of a king. She then encouraged the class to raise questions about Carter, the trail, the tomb and the king – these questions became the focus for the rest of the topic.

During the unit, children carried out a range of activities, including writing a diary entry for Howard Carter, in which they explained and discussed his thoughts and feelings about discovering the tomb. They also visited a Tutankhamun exhibition at a local museum. Children were engaged and fascinated by the topic. Much of the success of the unit could be put down to the initial curiosity raised by the use of objects and sources in the initial activity, although the elements of role-play and drama were also significant.

Artefacts

In history and geography, an object or artefact is usually a product shaped or made by a human being – natural objects (for example, a lump of pumice from a volcanic eruption) may be valuable for particular enquiries, but the key to the value of artefacts is generally the evidence of human action, intervention or interaction. Within the context of primary humanities, an artefact is usually an item of historical or cultural interest, which says something about its creator, users and the environment in which it was produced. Such objects or artefacts may be the outcome of archaeological endeavour, be a family heirloom or may have been deliberately created or collated, possibly including replicas, to support a particular investigation.

Artefacts from the recent past can be relatively easy to obtain from children's older relatives – a request for objects and documents from the 1960s or even the home front in the last war can yield a surprising number of disparate items that have been gathering dust in store cupboards and attics. Similarly, objects from distant places can be easily obtained from travellers for business or pleasure. Even insignificant and random objects from distant localities can help to make enquiries cogent and purposeful – travel tickets, menus, food wrappers, cultural souvenirs all contribute to making a distant place real, tangible and the location of everyday lives. Objects from the distant past and objects from places not often visited by travellers are obviously more difficult to obtain. Museum loan services can provide access to real objects from the distant past – the Grosvenor Museum in Chester, for example, loans small collections of Roman objects to schools for relatively inexpensive rates. Similarly, artefacts from localities in the developing world can be loaned from some DECs.

Rather than relying on others, a teacher may wish to collect and curate their own collection of objects, culled from junk shops, car boot sales and trips abroad. Collections of discarded items from visits to localities can be surprisingly engaging for young children, who can use them to begin to reconstruct the lifestyles and characteristics of distant places.

Figure 4.1 The running shoes used by the teacher in the case study

Learning with artefacts I: Running shoes

The teacher began the unit with a Year 2 class by passing a pair of 1920s running shoes around the circle. These shoes, belonging to a relative, were clearly old and had sharp spikes on the sole. The children discussed what they might be and what their possible purpose was. They had to justify their answers with reasons. Then the teacher gave the children a sticky label each. They had to think of a word to describe the shoes, which they then stuck around them. This was a very effective opening. It grabbed the children's attention and imagination. Many of the children straight away related the shoes to sport. Due to the shape and the spikes, the children thought they may have been used for rock climbing, football or hiking. The adjectives children used were interesting. One child described the shoes as looking tight. All the children believed that they were old, but were unable to date them. Answers ranged from two thousand years to five years old!

To help the children try and date the shoes, the teacher made a timeline. The timeline ranged from 1900 to 2000 with 1950 in the middle. The children were put into groups of three. Each group was given an event from the twentieth century, which they then had to plot on the timeline which had been put up on a wall outside. The teacher then went through the timeline and discussed whether events were in the correct place. This was an important task to try and develop children's chronological awareness. The teacher returned to the timeline throughout the unit.

In the next activity the children were shown a race from the film *Chariots of Fire*. The scene depicted Eric Liddell running in the 1924 Olympics. They were then shown the men's 100 metre final from the 2012 Olympics. The children identified the differences and similarities between the two races. The teacher asked the children if they could spot in either clip similar shoes to those that they had handled. They then discussed their observations and possible reasons for the changes over time.

The children made interesting observations. In particular that there were no black people running in the *Chariots of Fire* clip. This was a good introduction to the next lesson in which they looked at the achievements of Jesse Owens.

After comparing the clips, the children then had a go at dating the shoes. They had identified that shoes worn in the 1924 film clip were more similar to the shoes they had been looking at than the ones in the 2012 Olympics clip. Previously the children's estimates had ranged over 2000 years. A combination of using the timeline and the comparison activity had clearly had an effect.

The teacher opened the next lesson by attaching a label to the shoes with the words 'Property of Jesse Owens, 1936' written on it. The children then speculated about who Jesse Owens was and what the significance of 1936 was. From this the children produced questions. The children then used the internet to find answers. They discussed what they had found out about Jesse Owens and the 1936 Berlin Olympics.

The teacher then made links to PHSE, explaining how Jesse Owens had proved Hitler wrong by showing that white people are not better than black people. One child said that he read that Hitler left the stadium when Jesse Owens won one of his medals. The teacher explained that this was untrue. Jesse Owens led the way for more black athletes to compete in the Olympics. This point was emphasised by the teacher when he showed a video clip of Usain Bolt breaking the world record.

Throughout the sequence of lessons the teacher continued to return to and add to the timeline. Each time the children would order the events. This improved children's chronological awareness and it was an activity they enjoyed.

Strengths of artefacts

Artefacts can help young children to develop a sense of time and place. Many school-based resources are text based, whereas objects hold the same significance as language in terms of our everyday lives and basic needs. There are strong arguments in favour of the use of objects in terms of enhanced cognitive development and retention of knowledge and understandings (Dale's Cone of Experience, 1969); as Confucius said, 'I hear, I forget; I see, I remember; I do, I understand.' Handling objects is a multisensory experience and has the potential to elicit emotive responses and foster intellectual creativity within historical and geographical contexts, where content is often remote spatially and temporally. For example, objects may be used to support the study of distant localities in geography or key events and periods in history; learning where the use of imagination is key.

Learning with artefacts 2: A gramophone

While on school placement, a trainee teacher was asked to do a short history lesson with a group of Reception children on technology in the past. She decided to focus the activity on an old wind-up gramophone belonging to a relative. Before she revealed the gramophone to the class, she showed them the old, rather battered leather case it came in. Various suggestions were made by the children as to what they suspected to be inside. 'A suitcase' was the most popular suggestion, as the case had a handle and a silver clasp to open and lock it shut. When the lid was slowly opened, the children gasped in anticipation. 'What is it?' some asked. Others looked clueless. 'It's a CD player,' one said and this was agreed with by some others. The trainee told the children that the object is called a gramophone and it plays records. Questions and responses were asked such as 'How old is it?', 'Where is the plug?', 'Can we put CDs on it?' The children were told that it was about a hundred years old and was wound up to make it work, not plugged into an electric socket. The trainee showed the children a record which came from a section in the lid of the case. The children all called it a 'big CD'. As the trainee lifted the playing arm up and placed the needle onto the edge of the record, the children were fascinated to see what would happen next. 'What do you think will happen once I have wound up the lever?' she asked. Most of the children said music would play out of it. The trainee explained to the children that she had to be extremely careful with all the parts of the gramophone because it was very old and she held their suspense by informing them that the gramophone might not work. She wound the lever around ten times, with the children joining in with the counting, then moved the brake lever to the side and the record began to slowly spin around. The trainee placed the needle onto the record and a strange scratchy sound came out. The children loved it when it didn't work. 'Is that someone singing?', one child asked. 'Yes, the trainee replied, 'but it should sound nicer than that!' The children looked at the gramophone intently, trying to discover what the trainee had done wrong. It was very exciting. She tried once more, but let the record gather speed before placing the needle onto it. 'Wow!' was the reaction around the group. The beautiful voice of a female singer came from the small speaker on the gramophone. The children were amazed. Some girls started dancing to the music and everyone listened intently. This was an encounter with an object that these children would remember for a long time.

Limitations of artefacts

It is important to stress to children when working with artefacts and objects that they are not merely items of curiosity, but may hold special meaning or significance and thus integrity should be exercised; for example, when handling religious artefacts which relate to a particular time or place. It may be more appropriate for special or precious objects to be viewed as images or video footage.

It is something of a paradox that, although the kinaesthetic nature of objects and artefacts makes them highly appropriate as sources to use with young children, they are some of the most difficult sources to interpret without help. An old flat iron may be similar enough to a modern household item to make it meaningful, but many other items from the past will be impossible to identify and interpret without support. Storytelling and drama (see the Case Study, *Introducing Tutankhamun's Tomb* on page 61) are effective ways of addressing this issue and can help place unfamiliar artefacts into historical and cultural contexts which allow children to question and interpret.

There are also issues surrounding the reinforcement and promotion of stereotypes and misconceptions. Within the context of geographical enquiries this is to do with the degree to which the artefacts and resources are representative of the place being studied. In history, for example, a set of artefacts relating to life in Victorian times may be limited to one social group or region only. In geography, a set of artefacts relating to a locality in India may be highly stereotypical and non-representative of life in India today.

With the above points in mind, it is of paramount importance that children develop the confidence and ability to ask the right questions and to take a critical stance. Key skills needed to work effectively with artefacts comprise observation, questioning and recording.

Website

For history, the Nuffield Primary History Project materials that are located on the Historical Association website provide a wealth of ideas for using objects and artefacts in the classroom: www.history.org.uk/resources/primary_resource_3657_130.html

Maps and globes

A map is a two-dimensional representation of an area on a flat surface and is usually paper-based or has been generated digitally. It is a very important source of primary data for both historical and geographical investigations as well as being of vital significance for life in a twenty-first-century globalised society. Online maps can be more than just static documents – superimposing live shipping movements or flight information can bring the reality of global links and connections to life.

 Websites

www.flightradar24.com provides live flight data superimposed on maps at various scales.

www.marinetraffic.com/ais shows the positions and routes of ships throughout the world.

There is an extremely wide range of historical and contemporary maps available; the range spans from early depictions drawn by hand to interactive software such as *Google Earth*. The mapmaker or cartographer will choose a map projection depending on the area in question and the intended audience. The most accurate world map is a globe as this is a three-dimensional scale model of Earth.

Strengths of maps and globes

Maps, aerial photographs and globes represent a powerful visual source which can support enquiry-based learning. There is a wide range of maps and plans available. For example, maps used in primary settings may range from ground plans to oblique and aerial photographs and to more complex topographic and thematic maps and atlases. This is the inherent strength of maps; that they can be used to inform a wide range of geographical and historical enquiries, providing children with opportunities to analyse patterns in space and across time and to foster and develop a critical approach. This is of paramount importance as all maps are intrinsically biased depending on the original intentions of the mapmaker.

 To think about

Maps and their messages

Gather a collection of maps and plans from different sources – for example, Tourist Information Centres, shopping malls, nature reserves, Ordnance Survey maps – and compare the ways in which they convey spatial information. How is line and colour used? What information is included and what is missed out? How pictorial are the maps? How abstract are they? What is the bias of each map?

All maps present information selectively and with some form of bias. Ordnance Survey maps provide a wealth of cultural information, but very little commercial information – an OS map will show the location of a local museum or historic site, but not the nearest branch of a particular supermarket chain. Maps aimed at tourists may distort the relative size and significance of visitor attractions, so that they can be more easily found. A topographic map, such as the iconic London Underground map, will sacrifice accuracy, in terms of position and distance, for clarity and ease of use.

How would you use your collection of maps with primary children? What questions do the maps raise and what questions do they answer?

Using a range of maps together can also help children to develop key aspects of mapping such as perspective and representation. The use of oblique and aerial photographs alongside simple maps, for example, can help to develop these key concepts. Similarly, with respect to digital mapping, applications such as *Google Earth* and online tools, such as *Bing Maps* and *Google Street View* can aid the development of perspective and representation, as well as making cogent links between maps and the real world.

Historical maps may appear initially to be quite daunting sources for young children to use, but in fact many are easier to decipher than modern maps. Mapmakers in the seventeenth and eighteenth centuries, for example, had no set of conventional symbols to use, so their maps of towns and country estates are essentially pictorial sources and are highly accessible. Medieval maps of the world, such as Mappa Mundi in Hereford

Cathedral, are also essentially pictures showing very clearly the world view of their creators – there are many images of Mappa Mundi online and the British Library website (www.bl.uk) maintains an evolving online collection of mapping imagery, from ancient world maps to old town plans.

Limitations of maps and globes

As stated above, the strength of this type of resource lies in the fact that map content is driven by a specified purpose and audience. However, this means that children need to learn how to critically analyse historical and contemporary maps in terms of both validity and reliability. They also need to be taught the importance of corroborating one map source with another. This leads on to another potential limitation in that it is the use of an increasingly wide range of different sources and resources that facilitates progression and depth of understanding in historical and geographical enquiry. A variety of maps need to be explored within the context of a welter of related resources and for schools this clearly has resourcing implications.

Consideration also needs to be given to the fact that children need to be taught how to use maps by exploring various aspects of mapping such as perspective, representation, scale, direction and location. The sequence of learning should be based on these key concepts and activities need to be logically structured in terms of the age, ability and prior learning of the children in question. The temptation might be to teach these aspects in isolation – a worksheet on perspective where children are asked to draw an object from a 'bird's-eye view' or an exercise where symbols are decoded on a map of an unknown area. Such activities should be avoided, however, as mapping skills are best learned in the context of meaningful enquiries. Out of context, skills-based map activities may have a value for developing specific skills for particular enquiries, but generally they can be seen as the equivalent of learning to read using a phonics-based approach, but only decoding meaningless nonsense words.

 Websites

Using maps and plans in primary history on the Historical Association website: www.history.org.uk/resources/primary_resource_3657,3666_7.html

Old maps – an excellent source of historical mapping of the UK: www.old-maps. co.uk/index.html

Ordnance Survey educational resources and key concepts of mapping: www. ordnancesurvey.co.uk/oswebsite/education-and-research/teaching-resources/map-reading-made-easy.html

Photographs and images

Photographs and images are crucial primary sources within the context of humanities. A photograph is an image created by light falling on a light-sensitive surface and is usually created using a camera – increasingly, children engage with photographs digitally, either by creating them using digital cameras or by viewing them on computer screens, mobile devices and interactive whiteboards. There is still much to be gained from getting children to handle prints and construct meaning through physical engagement with printed photographs and images, however. Prints can be more easily annotated and extended by groups of children than digital images, although tablet devices now have a similar potential for small groups. Images in primary history may also include a variety of forms of artistry including impressions, paintings, sketches and rubbings. Portraits are a particularly interesting subset among paintings in that their status as commissioned works (usually by the subject of the portrait) can provide fascinating insights into the self-image and mindset of, usually, wealthy people in the past.

Strengths of photographs and images

Complementary to other visual resources and sources (such as maps), photographs and images also contribute to the development of the key concepts of time and place and can bring geography and history to life; they can capture the spirit of a time and place.

If seen as a form of discourse, rather like text, the photograph or image is interpreted in a variety of ways by the reader and it is through this process that meaning is established. As such, images are an excellent tool for promoting thinking skills and questioning approaches. The photograph or image should not be passively received, but be interrogated critically with content being related back to key theoretical ideas in humanities subjects (see Chapters 1 and 2, on inductive and deductive reasoning). This is crucial to the integrity of both history and geography teaching, where theories and models are continually tested and reviewed in the light of new cases and evidence: for example, analysing aerial views of a specific river and relating data back to the theory of river systems; discovering new evidence in a painting about an historical figure, which changes their story.

Try this activity

Biased images

Put yourself in the position of a photographer given a selective brief in relation to recording a locality. Take a short walk around a locality and, using a digital camera or camera phone, take a set of photographs that could be used to illustrate a tourist brochure or other literature to attract visitors. Download your images to a computer or upload them to an online service, such as *Flickr* or *Picasa*. Now go out and do the same walk again, but this time take a set of photographs that could be used in a report to attract funding to improve the locality or attract investment for environmental improvements. Download or upload this set of photos. Now, using the slideshow facility in your computer software or online service, run the sets of images as slideshows or image sequences.

How is the locality portrayed differently in the two slideshows? What features have you included or excluded from the two slideshows? How easy is it to produced biased sets of images that portray the same place in different ways?

Limitations of photographs and images

The problematic nature of photographs and images is rooted in the fact that they can never be neutral representations, despite their apparent ordinariness. This relates not only to the artists/photographers behind images, but also to the individual interpreting and reading them. Particular details may be accentuated or focused upon, excluded or downplayed. For example, a series of images produced by an aid agency about a distant locality may selectively focus on poverty and misery and in doing so not truly represent the location in question. Research evidence also points to developmental stages in children's ability to gain meaning from images, with young children often focusing on details, rather than taking in the whole picture.

⌨ Websites

Children in the five-to-seven age range in particular may need support to access information in visual images – see an action research report on research into children's developing visual literacy: http://geography.org.uk/download/GA_EYPPRRActionResearch4Pickford.pdf

Geographical Association: activities using images: www.geography.org.uk/resources/adifferentview/imagesandactivities/

Historical Association on using visual images: www.history.org.uk/resources/primary_resource_3657,3664_7.html

Written and printed sources

Written sources comprise a variety of texts, which may include private letters, diaries, memoirs, poems, novels and newspapers. Printed and written documentation represent an important source in both history and geography and an important maxim is to teach about the document type prior to using it within a specific enquiry.

A written source that is particularly useful for historical enquiries into life in the nineteenth and early twentieth centuries is the census. A general census has been conducted in this country every ten years since 1801. The first gathered only population figures for villages or towns. However, since 1851, details of the members of each household have been collected and recorded in enumerators' schedules. The most recent available census is for 1911. The main problem with their use is the illegibility of the handwriting of the period, although this can be addressed by transcription of parts of the records. Census extracts could be used individually or records from different years could be compared in order to trace developments over time. One of the most important implications is that, in investigating census materials, children will be finding out about real people and carrying out original research.

Strengths of written and printed sources

Written documents can provide an intimate insight into life in the past and across different locations. Documentation, such as poetry and creative writing, can give a highly personal portrait, capturing the spirit and culture of the time and place in which they were written. There is an emotional appeal in that well-chosen text engages and enables the reader to closely identify with life at that time or in that place. This is important for children who, due to their inherent egocentricity, need to identify with others in order to fully engage and develop their understandings about places and historical phenomena.

Figure 4.2 The blue plaque on Chester Town Hal

A blue plaque as a starting point

A group of trainee teachers was given the task of assembling a set of sources, using a local Record Office, which could be used to tell a story with Key Stage 2 children. They used a range of written documents, alongside maps and images, to tell the story of Chester Town Hall. Their starting point was the blue plaque on the Town Hall, which among other key facts tells the reader that the present building is a replacement for an earlier building which was destroyed by a fire in 1862. At Cheshire Archives, the trainees found images of the fire and a newspaper report from the *Chester Record* newspaper, written in florid Victorian language, telling the story of the destruction of the Exchange. One notable event during the fire was an injury to a local resident who was helping the hapless firefighters: Mr John Price of nearby Watergate Street was hit on the head by part of a falling flagpole and had to be helped home. The trainees were fascinated by this fact and wanted to find out more about Mr Price. Prompted by the education archivist, they consulted the census from the previous year (1861) to find out that Mr Price was a 57-year-old teacher of languages, with a wife and grown-up children, who lived at 41 Watergate Street.

He had two servants and came originally from Wales. But did he survive the injury? The census carried out ten years later in 1871 held the answer. Mr Price was still living with his family in Watergate Street in 1871, but his occupation had changed from a teacher of languages to a teacher of mathematics! Perhaps the blow on the head had had some effect?

The finished project showed clearly that a range of written documents, particularly Victorian census records, can bring a story to life through access to real people and their lives. Like all good enquiries, the project raised as many questions as it answered and produced a resource which continues to be used in some local schools.

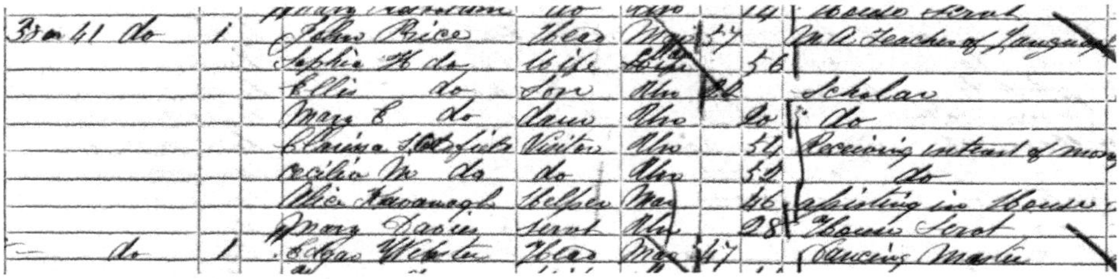

Figure 4.3 An extract from the 1861 census of Watergate Street in Chester, showing the Price household. On the night of the census, Mr John Price, his wife and children had two visitors. The handwriting obviously makes census documents quite challenging as sources, so they may need to be transcribed before they are used with younger children

Limitations of written and printed sources

Inevitably the limitations are rooted in the fact that documents may not have been written with a wider audience in mind and so contents may be biased, candid and highly subjective. For this reason, encouraging children to take a critical stance is essential to their work as primary geographers and historians. When and how documentation was authored is a key consideration. Motives relating to the society in which it was produced – political, religious, commercial – must all be taken into account.

There may also be issues concerning legibility and children's ability to access the content of the documentation. To overcome this limitation, it may be necessary to transcribe some documentation or use technology to facilitate access – for example, accessing nineteenth-century census documents using a simple flat-file database – remembering always to try to introduce children to the original, where possible.

Website

Historical Association on using printed and written sources: www.history.org.uk/ resources/primary_resource_3720_1.html

Audio: music

Music that is redolent of particular times and places can make a significant contribution to children's enquiries, providing insights into a range of cultural norms and traditions, as well as giving a sense of the soundtrack of ordinary lives. Although the musical tastes prevalent in cultures from the distant past can only be guessed at, more recent societies may have left clues in the form of instruments, notation, recordings or traditions passed down through the generations. Contemporary music from around the world can be accessed in many ways, ranging from online audio libraries to CD compilations from specialist music labels.

Strengths of music

As well as adding another sensory dimension to enquiries, musical forms, styles and traditions can help in finding answers to a range of questions, including those relating to entertainment, faith and communication. Forms of dance are inextricably linked to musical traditions in particular cultures; and music can provide clues to the mores, customs and physical expression prevalent in particular societies. Tudor court music, for example, exemplified by 'Greensleeves' (which was reputedly composed by Henry VIII himself), suggests sedate and stately dance styles whereas the rock 'n' roll music of the late 1950s suggests a very different type of physical response.

Limitations of music

Visual and tactile sources, in the form of images and instruments, are needed to complete the picture provided by audio evidence. The music of particular times and cultures may sound similar to modern styles, but be produced by very different instrumentation. It can also be a mistake to assume that musical styles and traditions from particular times and cultures are representative of popular tastes in those times and cultures. Traditional English folk music, for example, is culturally representative, but lacks mass appeal today.

Website

Putumayo produces CD compilations of music from a wide range of cultures and traditions. Some CDs are specifically aimed at children and teacher resources are available: www.putumayo.com/en/putumayo_kids.php

Audio: oral sources

People talking about their personal perspectives and experiences can provide cogent evidence to inform enquiries, especially investigations into recent history. Oral evidence from people who have travelled to distant places or have particular expertise on an issue can enliven geographical enquiries, which would otherwise depend on secondary source material. Accessing the views of others in the community will be an important part of any enquiry into a contentious local issue.

Strengths of oral sources

Child-led first-hand interviews with people can be powerful and moving experiences for all concerned. Whether recalling events during wartime or personal experiences in hostile environments, interviewees can respond directly to children's interests and needs. Recorded oral sources, especially audio recordings, will be more challenging for children, but well-chosen short extracts can still bring distant events or places to life through contact with the lived experiences of others. Video recordings will be more accessible, but some editing may still be necessary to ensure that speakers are responding to children's likely concerns and interests.

Limitations of oral sources

Academic historians tend to be quite sceptical about the value of oral history. They would argue that single oral accounts give only highly personal, usually biased and quite partial accounts. People recalling distant events and experiences will be explicitly or implicitly selective. Although shortcomings can be overcome by making interactions child-led and focused on children's questions and interests, personal accounts will require sensitive and tactful exploration of bias, accuracy and plausibility.

ICT: handling information

Many geographical enquiries provide opportunities for the development of data handling skills, either on or off the computer. Numerical data – for example, from a traffic survey or a simple weather station – can be quickly processed and presented by ICT tools, such as graphing programs, databases or spreadsheets. Mobile devices, such as tablets, allow children to enter and process data in the field. History provides fewer contexts for such activities, but specific tasks, such as the analysis of census data, are greatly enhanced by the use of database programs.

Strengths of ICT

ICT can help to make sense of large amounts of data, for example, a year's weather data from a distant location or census information from a large district. The use of ICT tools to display and analyse data greatly speeds up the process, giving more time for discussion and interpretation by children. ICT enables data (numbers) to be quickly turned into information: connections, relationships and frequencies.

Limitations of ICT

The graphs and charts that are quickly produced by appropriate software should not be seen as ends in themselves: children should be prompted, supported and scaffolded so that they identify the patterns and trends in graphical representations. The time saved by the use of ICT tools should be used to facilitate discussion, analysis and interpretation. The creation of graphical representations by hand is a necessary precursor to the use of ICT tools, so that children understand what software is doing when it turns columns of figures into colourful charts. Children also need to develop mathematical understandings about the use of appropriate chart types, for example, line graphs are only appropriate for displaying continuous data, such as temperature over time.

 Website

Age-appropriate educational data-handling software should be used to support the development of information-handling skills, before children encounter business-oriented packages, such as Microsoft *Excel* – for example, 2Simple software supplies *2Count* and *2Graph* to introduce computer-based graphing to children in Key Stage 1: www.2simple.com

ICT: Internet

The range and capacity of online sources provide a wealth of materials for almost all likely topics in the primary school. Precious historical sources, such as documents in the British Library or the National Archives, which previously could only be accessed by a few, can now be freely accessed by anyone with an internet-capable device. Some pre-packaged sets of sources are available to answer specific enquiry questions. Many local archives and record offices provide online access to some of their sources.

Strengths of online sources

Online resources are particularly appropriate for enquiries where answers or solutions may be contentious or debatable. Online materials are available from a huge range of sources, giving all sides of almost any debate or argument, for example, the views of proponents and opponents of wind farms as renewable energy resources. The wide range of sources allows children to compare and contrast different views and information. Interactive whiteboards and large screens allow online resources, such as videos and still images, to be easily shared with a whole class. Structured enquiries, or Web Quests, can be set up to enable children to research and explore in a focused and safe manner. Web Quests give the teacher more control over children's Web-based research and a clearly defined structure for investigation, within constructivist principles.

The internet can also provide synchronous or asynchronous access to people in distant places or experts on a range of subjects, either by videoconferencing or chat/e-mail facilities. Blogging and other interactive tools (sometimes called Web 2.0 technologies) can provide formats for online communication and feedback, perhaps around a set of images, or can provide audiences for communicating enquiry findings. Such tools are also useful for establishing and maintaining home–school links. Web 2.0 tools allow children to upload resources for sharing and to communicate using a wide range of multimedia tools. Social networking has huge potential for transforming learning through communication and dialogue with others.

Limitations of online sources

Although there are many reputable, well-researched online sources available, it is still true that almost anyone can set up a website and all sites should be treated with some caution before satisfactory answers are found to basic evaluation questions. Web-based sources also provide easy opportunities for plagiarism. Asking children to make handwritten notes can avoid the temptation to copy and paste. The preparation of Web Quests can be time-consuming and the constantly changing nature of the Web may mean some online resources quickly become obsolete, are removed or change their URLs. Once created, a Web Quest needs constant checking and updating to make sure it remains functional and relevant. The use of Web 2.0 tools needs to be undertaken within the framework of a well-understood acceptable use policy. Liaison with parents and carers is vital to ensure that children are aware of e-safety issues when researching and communicating outside, as well as inside, schools and settings. Web 2.0 has tremendous potential for learning, but also potential for abuse by children (unwitting or otherwise) and others.

 Websites

National Archives Lessons: guided enquiries using sources: www.nationalarchives.gov.uk/education/lessons.htm

Documents from the British Library presented chronologically in an interactive timeline: www.bl.uk/learning/histcitizen/timeline/historytimeline.html

Rationale and tools for making Web Quests from Professor Bernie Dodge, the originator of the Web Quest idea: http://webquest.org/index.php

Quadblogging is a means by which groups of children – usually four, hence the name – in distant localities can communicate and comment on a chosen theme or enquiry: http://quadblogging.net

Web 2.0 sites with teacher facilities for creating class accounts:

- Primary Blogger
  http://primaryblogger.co.uk
- Glogster: a tool for making online interactive, multimedia posters
  http://edu.glogster.com
- Timetoast: interactive timelines for presenting information chronologically
  www.timetoast.com
- Edmodo: social network for a class to share notes, links or files
  www.edmodo.com
- Diipo: social network for a class to blog, share notes, links or files.
  http://diipo.net

ICT: simulations

ICT can provide access to distant locations in time and space and model concepts and ideas, through games-based learning, animations and/or virtual reality (VR) applications. Processes and developments, which may occur over long periods or in inaccessible places, can be modelled – for example, issues encountered by invaders and settlers. Augmented Reality (AR) – using computers or mobile devices to add additional sensory input or information to real-world experiences – offers great potential for engaging learners in investigations in the field. Software on tablets and smartphones can add information to the view through a camera, by linking internet information sources to locations identified by GPS. Marker-based AR systems, using QR codes read by smartphone cameras or webcams, can link features or objects to Web-based information and, in some cases, create the illusion of 3-D objects on the computer screen.

Strengths of simulations

Immersive panoramas using Quicktime™ VR provide opportunities to vicariously visit and explore distant or inaccessible places. Simulations and adventures which use the motivating and familiar conventions of gaming enable children to engage in quite sophisticated decision making and problem solving in both historical and geographical contexts, for example, choices made by Viking raiders or choices relating to renewable and non-renewable energy sources to provide power for a town. Animations can speed up lengthy processes to make them intelligible and accessible to children – for example, coastal erosion in physical geography. Although in their infancy, AR systems can add an extra dimension to exploration of trails, localities or historic sites. Software is available for children to create AR-enhanced trails. Although devices for AR are expensive, many children will possess smartphones that have the capability to run AR applications or apps. Although marker-based systems have little more than novelty value at the time of writing, there is huge potential for learning, for example, bringing a 3-D version of a precious artefact from a museum into the classroom.

Limitations of simulations

Misconceptions may be reinforced by simplification of complex issues or speeding up of lengthy processes in some simulations. Working with AR systems requires preparation and (at the time of writing) some technical skill. Teachers may be reluctant to let children loose with expensive equipment in some locations. Although children may have personal devices capable of AR activities, their use raises ethical and e-safety issues.

 Websites

360-degree panoramas of places and events worldwide using Quicktime™ VR technology: www.fullscreenqtvr.com

BBC 'Viking Quest' interactive game: www.bbc.co.uk/history/ancient/vikings

'Power Up!' interactive game about energy choices: www.sciencenetlinks.com/interactives/powerup.html

BBC Rivers and Coasts resource includes several animated simulations of physical processes: www.bbc.co.uk/schools/riversandcoasts

Layar is software for displaying information from the internet on a mobile device's camera screen: www.layar.com

Rainforest life – AR puts a slender loris in the palm of your hand! www.zsl.org/zsl-london-zoo/exhibits/rainforestlife

 **Summary**

Within this chapter, a range of sources and resources have been analysed in terms of strengths and limitations. High-quality and engaging resources are fundamental to an enquiry-based approach where children are thinking, questioning and piecing together the evidence. Children need to be taught how to use such sources effectively, encouraged to take a critical stance and to corroborate one source with another.

CHAPTER 5

ENQUIRY IN PRACTICE IN HISTORY AND GEOGRAPHY

By the end of this chapter you will:

- understand that the use of open, investigative questioning is at the core of the enquiry approach in humanities and that this type of questioning challenges children to tackle real issues and problems – to speculate, debate and make connections;
- recognise that enquiry in the humanities involves a number of teaching and learning strategies;
- understand that thinking skills and strategies are the tools of enquiry in the humanities;
- be aware of a number of practical examples of enquiries in history and geography.

Since 1999, the National Curriculum has emphasised, in addition to the acquisition of subject-based knowledge and skills, the enquiry approach and the processes of learning, highlighting creativity and thinking skills. It explicitly stated that geography and history should be taught through enquiry, at both Key Stages 1 and 2. Enquiry skills involve the children in creating personal and shared understanding of the world around them and enables 'pupils to ask relevant questions, to pose and define problems, to plan what to do and how to research, to predict outcomes and anticipate consequences, and to test conclusions and improve ideas' (DfEE/QCA, 1999: 22). However, over the years, the meaning of 'enquiry', in both history and geography, has been interpreted in many different ways by schools and individual teachers, which has led to a degree of confusion and inconsistency in approach. Teachers have to be secure in the enquiry-based approach to learning because, for this method of learning to be effective, it has to be well taught and modelled by the teacher.

Enquiry-based teaching is not simply about looking for and arriving at the right answer, because sometimes there isn't one: instead it requires the teacher to allow for a range of answers and to teach the children that often no one answer is 'right'. This approach gives children confidence to work towards solutions to questions, problems and issues.

It's *not* about covering the content, it's about uncovering the learning.

(Anonymous)

Many teachers are more comfortable with the traditional approach to learning, which is teacher centred, focused on content and has less emphasis on the development of skills, either subject-specific skills or the more universal skills of learning, or on the promotion of enquiring attitudes. In the traditional approach, the teacher is the font of all knowledge, the children are passive receivers of this information and much of the assessment is focused on 'recall' and the importance of the one correct answer.

The process of enquiry is in line with recent research on how children learn best, the new approaches to effective, creative and personalised learning and developing thinking skills.

What does enquiry in history and geography mean for children?

Enquiry-based learning builds on the children's prior knowledge, understanding, values, beliefs and preconceptions about the world, develops their curiosity and supports them in making sense of the world for themselves. Enquiry is based on the children's desire to know and supports them in developing understanding, through questions and analysis. In geography, even the very youngest children have their own personal experiences of places and environments and in history they have a growing interest in their own family and local histories. Teaching approaches must draw out and work with children's pre-existing knowledge and understanding and ensure that the pupils' 'thinking' is visible and central to the learning.

Memorising facts and information is not the most important skill in today's world.

> The meaning of knowing has shifted from being able to remember and repeat information to being able to find and use it. The goal of education is better conceived as helping students develop the intellectual tools and learning strategies needed to acquire the knowledge necessary to think productively.
>
> Nobel Laureate Herbert Simon 1996

In the primary schools, there has been a long tradition of children undertaking 'topic work' and research. For decades children have been given homework tasks or sent to the library to 'find out about' some historical or geographical topic. This tedious ritual led to a lot of information gathering and rote copying but little analysis or thought.

The content and knowledge bases for subjects such as history and geography are constantly expanding and a phenomenal amount of facts, information and data is readily available, using simple search strategies on the internet. No one can ever learn every fact, but, through the process of enquiry, children can be encouraged to develop the investigative skills and enquiring attitudes necessary to develop a greater understanding of the interconnectedness of the natural and man-made global village in which they live, learn, communicate and work. The enquiry approach is one way of preparing our children for their lives in the future; lives which will be characterised by rapid technological progress and expansion, globalisation, social and cultural change.

Enquiry implies a 'need or want to know' and it is through this approach that children are encouraged to become lifelong learners. However, enquiry-based learning is definitely not a return to the child-centred permissive education of the 1970s.

> What counts is not what the children know today but what they can do with it tomorrow.
>
> (Anonymous)

Enquiry-based learning through the humanities encourages schools to focus on developing the kinds of educational experience appropriate for young people growing up in the twenty-first century age of globalisation.

To think about

With a fellow student, think about the attitudes to learning, skills and ways of working you would like to encourage children to develop. Does your list match the attitudes to learning, skills and ways of working fostered by enquiry-based learning in history and geography listed below?

Enquiry-based learning in history and geography encourages and develops children's

- curiosity and inquisitiveness about their own experiences and everyday lives;
- ability to make sense of the world for themselves;
- thirst for knowledge and understanding;
- confidence to develop their own ideas and to take the risk, in a safe, supportive environment, where the challenge is high but the threat is low;
- confidence and ability to pose problems and ask relevant questions;
- ability to recognise issues that they would like to pursue and explore;
- awareness that sources, artefacts, records and events may be observed, examined, scrutinised and evaluated from many different perspectives;
- confidence to use technology to enhance learning;
- awareness that knowledge changes over time as people challenge, shape and contribute to it.

Through historical enquiry children are taught how to find out about past events and people who lived in the past. This involves a number of teaching strategies including questioning, hypothesising, planning investigations, researching, information handling and study skills. It requires children to find historical evidence from a range of sources. They have to learn how to use and question historical sources such as artefacts, paintings, pictures and museums, as well as film and Web-based resources. At primary level, each historical theme needs opening through questions, rather than through content. An artefact, historical document or a visit can be used as a stimulus to capture the interest and imagination of the children, from which they can create a number of enquiry questions.

To undertake any historical enquiry, children need to be familiar with using different sources of evidence, both primary and secondary sources. They need to be able to decide which things are most useful to them for examining the past and which are not. Children need to be able to look at a source of evidence and decide on its relevance to their particular enquiry (does it relate to the period of history in the enquiry and the agreed research focus), its reliability (can the source be relied upon to give accurate factual information about the past) and the richness of the source (does the source give lots of detail about what it was really like at that time?).

Simple sorting activities, where the children sort evidence in order of reliability, helps them develop an understanding of the accuracy of sources. A simple sorting activity is illustrated below.

 Try this activity

- Provide the children with a set of sources of evidence, such as a diary extract, photographs, painting, film archive, artefact, non-fiction reference book, website, fiction film, newspaper article, letter, etc. Ask the children to work in small groups to sort them in order of reliability. Children feed back and discuss findings.

- Ask the children to work in the same groups and this time to order the sources according to which might give the richest evidence about life in the past. In this activity, the children carefully consider and deliberate the reliability of a source against the richness of detail about real life that it might offer.

- For example: If the children were investigating 'Who were the Vikings?' through subsidiary questions such as 'What were the Vikings really like?', 'Where did they come from?' and 'Why did they come?', ask the children which three sources of evidence they would select and why.

Children need to gain an appreciation of the difference between source and evidence. They need to understand that it is their role as historians to turn the source into evidence for a particular question or questions, through the enquiry process, questioning the source and interpreting the information and data they derive from the source.

Enquiry and questioning

The only dumb question is a question you don't ask.
(Paul Macready, inventor (1925–2007)

Questions are part of traditional teaching. However, in this type of teaching, the teacher is usually the questioner and the questions are often closed, seeking factual information and involving a right or wrong answer. In the enquiry process, the questioning techniques, purposes and level of questioning used are quite different. Enquiry in history and geography also requires the teacher to allow for a range of answers and to teach children that often no one answer is 'right'. Answers to enquiry questions cannot be found. Children construct their own answers and make their own sense of the information they have collected.

> I keep six honest serving men,
> They taught me all I knew:
> Their names are What and Why
> and When
> and How and Where
> and Who.
>
> Rudyard Kipling,
> 'The Elephant's Child', *Just So Stories* (1902)

The effective use of open, probing questioning is at the heart of the enquiry approach in humanities and underpins the whole of the teaching and learning process. Good enquiry questions spark the children's curiosity and sense of wonder, because the questions usually stem from something which really matters to the children themselves and which they want to know more about and understand. The children are motivated to search for innovative and imaginative responses.

Closed questions seeking factual information are not automatically 'bad' questions, as they get the children to look closely at sources for facts and answers, but need complementary questions, which are more open and reflective in nature. Open questioning engages the children in activities that help them actively put forward further questions, investigate, solve problems and draw conclusions about the world around them. Teachers having plans full of stimulating enquiry questions is not enough to develop children's understanding of enquiry, if all the posing of questions and structuring of enquiry is done by the teacher. Children need to learn to frame their own enquiry questions, as shown in Table 5.4, later in the chapter. Initially, this needs to be taught, encouraged and modelled by the teacher generating enquiry questions. An effective teacher encourages the children to identify and ask their own subsidiary questions, as these will help them answer the main enquiry question.

Developing enquiry through questioning

Questions supply enthusiasm and vitality to primary history and this drives the process of learning. Teachers, modelling ways of questioning and analysing sources, will help children develop their own good historical enquiry skills. Good history teaching encourages children to generate their own questions and hypotheses and to piece together the information to create a fuller picture. Children need to be able to scrutinise the evidence and reach their own conclusions. They must also develop the confidence to articulate their conclusions and views from an informed position.

The question starters, illustrated in Table 5.1, are linked to the key concepts in history. They provide support and scaffolding for developing effective, rigorous and focused enquiry questions.

Table 5.1 Question starters to support the generation of enquiry questions linked to key concepts in history

Question starters	Link to historical key concepts
How did . . . e.g. How did life change . . . ? Why were . . . ? What were the differences . . . ? What made . . . ? Was life in . . . always . . . ?	Continuity and change: • develop an understanding of change over time and continuity by exploring similarities and differences between the past, the present and/or other periods of history • debate the impact of these changes • search for the evidence of continuity (uninterrupted or incremental development) or evidence of change (a clear break with the past, e.g. revolutions)
Why did . . . ? What were the effects . . . ? Why do we remember . . . ?	Cause and effect • investigate and discuss the causes and effects of past events and actions and how these have resulted in changes that affect people's lives and communities • learn to differentiate between causes and effects that are long-term, short-term or triggers

When did . . . live/take place? Which object is older? How do you know? Which event/activity/clothing is the oldest/newest?	**Time and chronology** • distinguish between the past, present and future • begin to develop time-related vocabulary • explore historical sequences, by placing objects, pictures and events in time sequences • record information about people and events in the past using simple timelines
How do we know . . . ? What can . . . tell us about . . . e.g. What do the songs/paintings/letters, etc. tell us about . . . ? Who can tell us most about . . . ? Why did . . . ? Why is it so difficult to find out about . . . .?	**Using evidence** • examine and ask questions about a range of simple historical evidence, e.g. photographs, pictures, objects, memories of older people, buildings, stories and songs, etc. • distinguish between fictional accounts in stories, myths and legends and real people and events in the past • summarise information and make simple deductions from different sources of evidence
Does . . . tell us the truth about . . . ? Why do people disagree/still argue about . . . ? Was . . . a hero/villain as portrayed? What's the story behind . . . ? Why have such different stories been told about . . . ? What was so important about . . . ? Why was . . . a failure/so successful?	**Synthesis, interpretation and communication** • use evidence and imagination to reconstruct elements of the past • understand that historians base their arguments on historical evidence, discover the truth by questioning and weighing up the differing evidence drawn from a variety of perspectives • communicate an awareness and understanding of stories, people and events from the past in a variety of ways, through oral language, writing, drama, modelling, other media including artwork, information and communication technologies, etc.
What was it like in/for . . . ? How do you think . . . felt when . . . ?	**Empathy** • imagine and discuss the feelings, motives and points of people in the past (to empathise, the children need to lose the prejudices and expectations of their own time and take on the attitudes and understanding of a past age)
Why was . . . so important to the . . . people? What was so important about . . . ? What lay behind . . . ?	**Features of societies:** 'First order' concepts that help us to understand historical trends and patterns as well as specific events. • concepts such as 'feudalism', 'nationalism', 'communism', 'revolution' and 'democracy'

Examples of overarching enquiry questions in history

Children are captivated by questions that provide a sense of mystery or intrigue about an aspect of the past.

- How did the Ancient Egyptians build the pyramids?
- What is a 'civilisation'? Who are the Aztecs? How did the Aztec society function?
- How does the Aztec calendar work? Compare the Aztec calendar with other calendars.
- How was Stonehenge built and what was it used for?
- Why were the Olympic Games so important to the Ancient Greeks?
- Who were the Vikings and what were they really like?
- What was life like in an Anglo-Saxon settlement?
- How much can we find out about people's daily lives in Roman Britain?
- Why did the Romans want to come to Britain?
- What made Elizabeth I so powerful?
- Why did Henry VIII marry so many times?
- What was life like for poor/rich children in Victorian times?
- What did the great Victorians achieve?
- Who was responsible for the Great Fire of London?
- How has life in our locality changed in the last 150 years?
- Have the new technologies changed the way we live in the last 50 years?

There have been many attempts to devise a definite set of geographical enquiry questions. In 1989, Michael Storm, in his article 'The five basic questions for primary geography' (Storm, 1989) suggested five basic questions. Over the years, variations of these questions have been suggested, as well as subsidiary questions (see Table. 5.2).

Table 5.2 Five basic enquiry questions in geography (after Storm) and subsidiary geographical questions

Key geographical enquiry questions	
Storm's basic questions	Subsidiary questions
What is this place like?	• Where is this place? • What do you expect the place to be like? • What is the place actually like? • What does this place look like?
Why is this place as it is?	• What made this place as it is? • Who lives here, and why? • Why do people visit this place? • What journeys do people make? • What jobs do people do? • What do people do in their spare time (leisure)? • Can the environment be improved? If so, how? • What services are there? • Does tourism affect this place? If so, how?
How is this place connected to other places?	• What links does this place have with other places? • How does this place interact with other places? • What global connections does this place have?
How is this place changing?	• Is this place changing? If so, why? • How do people use and care for the environment? • What issues affect the people who live there? • What are the views of the people who live there? • Who decides what should happen in this place?
What would it feel like to be in this place?	• What is it like to live in this place? • Why is this place special? • What are the main similarities and differences between this place and where we live?

Examples of overarching enquiry questions in geography

• How is my place changing?
• How are we affected by the seasons?

- How do rivers alter the landscape?
- How are coasts affected by erosion?
- How might Cliff Top Hotel be affected by coastal erosion?
- How am I connected to the world?
- What might happen to this place in the future?
- What are the problems facing the children of . . . following a natural disaster (e.g. tsunami, flood, hurricane)?
- Should a landfill site/waste incinerator/wind turbine be built here?
- Why is tourism affecting rare animals? What actions should be taken to protect them?
- What does it mean to be British?
- How is farming affected by the environment?
- What is the future for our woodlands and forests?

As discussed in Chapter 1, good enquiry questions are at the top of Blooms' Taxonomy (Blooms et al., 1956). They require children to evaluate and appraise, make careful choices between options, with the choice being based on clearly stated criteria; to synthesise, create or invent; or to analyse and examine, developing a thorough understanding through adept questioning. Blooms' categorisation may be used as a framework for planning units of work. For example, Blooms' taxonomy may be used to plan a unit of work, at Key Stage 2, on India (Table 5.3). By using the Blooms' taxonomy, the higher-order skills are activated through the questioning. In this example, the activities to develop geographical understanding, skills and knowledge include some thinking strategies and activities, such as 'Collective Memory', 'Living Graph', 'Odd One Out' and 'Mystery' as illustrated on the National Curriculum Thinking Skills posters from the Key Stage 3 Strategy (DfES, 2005).

Climate change enquiry

The effects of climate change are felt all over the world, having sudden and marked impact on all our lives and the lives of others. There is now very strong evidence and almost universal agreement that significant recent global warming can't be explained just by natural causes. The changes seen over recent years, and those predicted for the next century, are considered to be mainly the result of human behaviour.

Rising global temperatures and changes in weather patterns increase

Table 5.3   Let's look at India using Blooms' taxonomy as a planning tool

Blooms' taxonomy	Activities to develop geographical understanding, skills and knowledge
Remembering (knowledge) Factual answers, recall and recognition *Translate, outline*	List the capital city, other major cities, rivers and mountains, surrounding seas and oceans. Use 'Collective Memory' activity to learn about the physical features of India. Describe what happens at one of India's religious festivals/celebrations. 'India is a land of many contrasts.' Make alphabet book for a young child, illustrating the contrasts.
Understanding (comprehension) Translating, interpreting, showing understanding *Translate, outline, restate, interpret, summarise*	Use 'Collective Memory' activity to learn about the seasons and climate of India. Describe in your own words, with diagrams, the seasons and the climate of India. Describe traditional ingredients used in cooking and include a recipe for an Indian meal of your choice. Use 'Living Graph' strategy to review 'a year in the life of a rice farmer in India'.
Applying Using information gained in other (familiar) situations *Show how, illustrate, construct, use*	Make a list of other major mountain ranges in the world. Use 'Odd One Out' strategy to look at physical features. What instructions would you give a person making chapatti or a Diva lamp? Draw a diagram to explain the growing of rice.
Analysing Break into parts to examine more closely *Compare, contrast, separate*	Compare and contrast life in a village in India with life in a city in India. Create and use 'Mystery' strategy. Compare and contrast transport used in rural/urban India with transport used in rural/urban Britain.
Synthesis Combine information with new situations to create new products, ideas, etc. *Create, invent, design, improve*	Develop a dance based on the monsoon and the River Ganges. Produce a menu for an Indian banquet for four people and/or make a mild curry. Make a representation of the mountain environment and/or rice growing areas through collage. Write a poem and/or song to celebrate the coming of the monsoon.
Evaluating Judge, use criteria *Rank, substantiate, agree, validate, assess*	Evaluate the effectiveness of the aid agency work in empowering farmers to diversify and grow different food and cash crops. When the monsoon finally arrives, who is likely to appreciate the rain and water and who is likely to consider it a nuisance?

the frequency and intensity of extreme weather conditions like storms and heatwaves, which cause disasters in different parts of the world. Children are regularly exposed, through TV news reports, newspaper articles and the internet, to unbelievable suffering and loss of human life caused by the impact of climate change. An enquiry into climate change may start with the teacher generating an overarching enquiry question such as 'What impact does climate change have on some localities throughout the world?'

During the enquiry, the children need time for thinking and discussing. They need the opportunity to research and investigate ideas, challenge their own thinking and draw their own conclusions. Children start to generate their own questions and lines of enquiry, particularly in response to images they see on TV news programmes. They might ask questions such as: Where is this place? What has happened? Why has it happened? What causes climate change? Does climate change matter? Is there anything we can do about climate change to prevent further disasters?

 Try this activity

A sample of activities the children may undertake during this enquiry include the following.

- Ask the children, in groups, to carry out research on what climate change is and how it is caused, using simple search engines on the internet, non-fiction books, newspaper articles and extracts, etc.

- In the same groups, ask the children to sort evidence into two piles, one pile for 'facts' and the other 'opinion'. Each group selects a statement to read out to the rest of the class. The other groups have to decide whether the statement is 'fact' or 'opinion'.

- Using simple search engines on the internet, non-fiction books, newspaper articles and extracts, etc., ask the children, in groups, to carry out research on the places that have been affected, as a result of climate change, by such disasters as flooding, drought, avalanche, etc. Ask the children to locate the places on a map or globe.

- Following this, ask the children to create a presentation about one of the places that has been affected by climate change. Each group then presents to the other groups.

- Ask the children to take on different roles and write a statement about climate change, for example, in the role of a farmer, a holidaymaker, a recycling company, people living in different places affected by climate change, etc.

Enquiry cycle in history and geography

The role of the teacher in the enquiry process in history and geography has many aspects but that of facilitating children's learning is one of the most important. As the children become more confident with the enquiry process and take ownership of it, so the teacher's facilitation role will increase. Through the enquiry process, the teacher will support the children, giving them the confidence to share their ideas, work together as a group and value each other's unique contributions. Table 5.4 (overleaf) indicates the role of the teacher from the stage where the teacher initiates and structures the enquiry (focused) through to 'pupil-initiated' enquiry, where the children come up with their own enquiry questions and problems (facilitated). In Table 5.4, the developing role of the children is also illustrated.

Enquiry must not be a 'bolt-on' or one-off activity divorced from the rest of the term's work. The enquiry has to fit within the long-term plan and must be a repeatable process, 'question, hypothesis, testing, reformulation of hypothesis', which the children are able to use and reuse with increasing confidence and independence. Enquiry learning puts the learner at the centre of an active learning process, and the resources are prepared or aligned to support the learner. The teacher also becomes a learner by finding out more about the learner and the process of enquiry learning.

The enquiry process must be established and communicated to the children (Table 5.5, page 98).

From the start of the enquiry, children need to know exactly what's expected of them and what will be assessed. Skills which may be assessed in an historical or geographical enquiry might include: enquiry skills; basic skills; subject-specific skills; knowledge and understanding; research skills, including the use of technology to support enquiry; information-processing skills (from observations to synthesis); team skills; project management skills; presentation skills. This list is not exhaustive and will be different for other enquiries and children of different ages.

Enquiry and thinking skills

Thinking skills (information processing, reasoning, enquiry, creative thinking and evaluation) and strategies are the tools of enquiry and complement the six key skills, which help children improve their learning and performance (communication; application of number; information technology; working with others; improving own learning and performance; problem solving).

Table 5.4 The changing roles of teachers and children in developing enquiries

	FOCUSED	FRAMED	FACILITATED
T E A C H E R	Teacher:	Teacher:	Teacher:
	• initiates and structures the enquiry	• helps children to identify good ideas, questions or problems and agrees with them their focus for enquiry	• actively encourages children to come up with their own questions, problems and enquiry, i.e. working towards 'pupil-initiated' enquiry.
	• provides the context, questions and focus for enquiry	• helps children to plan their own short enquiries, usually in small groups	• creates a supportive environment with high challenge and low threat
	• designs activities and materials to help children share ideas and to further develop questioning	• supports the enquiry	• creates a safe environment to take risks
	• creates a supportive environment of high challenge and low threat	• creates a supportive environment with high challenge and low threat	• facilitates the enquiry, providing support and guidance when requested
	• creates a safe environment to take risks	• creates a safe environment to take risks	• helps to locate resources requested by children
	• models the process of enquiry	• assists children in the use of the enquiry model scaffold and ways of recording the enquiry	• supports children in reviewing information more critically and asking questions
	• provides scaffolds of the process of enquiry, taking the children through each stage of enquiry	• advises children on sources of information, providing support in validating the different sources of evidence	• supports children's communication skills
	• ensures that resources, artefacts and reference materials are available, including access to the internet	• provides and helps to locate resources, artefacts and reference material, including use of the internet, requested by children	• helps children to identify relevant audiences for their work
	• supports children in reviewing the validity of different sources of evidence	• encourages children to use prior knowledge and skills	• assesses children's progress thoroughly through dialogue and written feedback
	• supports children in developing skills in information gathering, analysis and organisation of evidence	• discusses work with the children regularly, offering guidance, ideas and advice	
	• helps children develop confidence in communicating their findings to others		

	FOCUSED	FRAMED	FACILITATED
C H I L D R E N	Children: • describe their experiences and ask questions • gather information from a range of resources and sources, including library books, the internet, their peers and home • discriminate between factual and popular beliefs and folk law • make use of different subject skills and knowledge, often in combination • collaborate in small groups • work on different presentation and communication formats	Children: • in groups and individually, take more responsibility for deciding on the focus of their enquiry • use different resources and types of knowledge • use a variety of research skills, including the use of ICT and library-based resources • become more able to identify authoritative/ reliable/honest sources from others • become confident communicating to audiences in a range of formats • reflect on their contributions and revise in the light of contribution of others	Children: • pose problems, ask questions and recognise issues to explore • define their own enquiry, identify the stages in an effective enquiry • carry out the enquiry systematically • collaborate with others • ask why and how things are the way they are • recognise when they have collected the relevant information that either answers a question or (dis)proves the validity of an idea • interrogate sources of evidence and are critical about how information is produced and for what purposes • look at things from a range of perspectives • appreciate and recognise that different people have different ideas about things • propose solutions to problems and questions • communicate in a range of formats and to different audiences, the learning that has emerged

Table 5.5 Establishing and communicating the enquiry process to children

ENQUIRY PROCESS	THE TEACHER'S ROLE IN SUPPORTING CHILDREN THROUGH THE ENQUIRY PROCESS
ACTIVATING PRIOR KNOWLEDGE AND EXPERIENCES CREATING A NEED TO KNOW	Ask: discuss with children what they already know about the topic, through their own experiences. Link: use the children's personal connection to the learning (topic), as this develops the children's curiosity and increases motivation and perseverance. Decide: how to 'hook' the children at the start of the enquiry. Is the focus of interest and relevance to the children?
ESTABLISHING THE ENQUIRY ENQUIRY QUESTION/FOCUS/HYPOTHESIS	Develop: a broad overarching enquiry question, from which children can develop subsidiary enquiry questions. Question: is the enquiry question rigorous and motivating? Decide: what aspects of historical/geographical knowledge, skills and understanding will be the particular focus of the enquiry?
BACKGROUND INFORMATION Children need a knowledge base so they can develop meaningful and relevant enquiries within the broad overarching problem/topic area.	Facilitate: children's background research, providing rich sources of information and resources, such as photographs, expert witnesses, personal accounts, stories, video clips, artefacts, etc. This base will enable the children to create a 'big picture' understanding of the broad topic area, and then to select specific enquiry interests.
LEARNING OUTCOMES AND ASSESSMENT From the start of the enquiry, children need to know exactly what's expected of them and what will be assessed.	Define: outcomes for which children will be accountable, i.e. what is going to be assessed. Incorporate: ongoing, meaningful peer and teacher assessment. Ensure: challenging expectations for children of varying abilities.

ESTABLISH AND COMMUNICATE THE ENQUIRY FRAMEWORK TO THE CHILDREN
Children need to see models of what it is they are being asked to do and be given supporting structures/scaffolds, which provides a foundation for their work, but doesn't limit their creativity.
	Model the enquiry
	  (a) state problem/question
	  (b) develop proposition which can be argued
	  (c) provide background information
	  (d) support proposition with: facts, statistics, examples, expert authority, logic and reasoning
	  e) propose solutions and action ideas
	Provide: supporting structures/scaffolds/frameworks.
	Re-emphasise the enquiry model.

UNDERTAKE INVESTIGATION AND ENQUIRIES, TESTING HYPOTHESIS USING DATA AND SOURCES	Facilitate: support children in outlining further focused questions within broader enquiry. Facilitate: ask questions to help children refine their thinking, guide their research, select and use information.
COMPARE, INTERPRET, ANALYSE AND MAKE SENSE OF THE INFORMATION	Facilitate: support the children in using their evidence to draw conclusions, offer explanations, consider, respond and debate alternative viewpoints and develop arguments.
PRESENT AND COMMUNICATE FINDINGS AND EXPLANATIONS	Facilitate: refer children back to expected outcomes and enquiry framework to create alignment between their presentations and intended outcomes. Facilitate: provide a forum for children to communicate their understanding through engaging presentations/end products. Facilitate: provide opportunity for children to connect their learning to specific, informed and responsible action.
REFLECT ON LEARNING AND EVALUATE	Facilitate: encourage children to reflect on what worked and what didn't and what they would do differently next time. Teacher also reflects on what worked and what didn't, and what they would do differently next time.

Fundamental to developing a thinking culture is the effective use of open, probing questioning to help raise children's curiosity and make them search for original responses. Children ask questions, articulate their thinking and discuss the problem or issue. Children discuss and evaluate their own learning *(metacognition)* and are encouraged to think about the process of *how they know what they know.*

Edward de Bono's 'Six Thinking Hats' tool (De Bono, 1992) provides an important and powerful technique to support children to think together more effectively. Instead of trying to do everything all at once, the historical or geographical enquiry question can be viewed from a number of different viewpoints, by breaking down the thinking into segments.

According to De Bono, the human brain thinks in six distinct ways (states). These states can be identified and planned for use in a structured way, so enabling children to develop strategies for thinking about particular issues. The six distinct thinking states are identified and assigned a coloured hat, the hats being used as symbols for each way of thinking. So, when everyone is wearing the same colour hat, everyone thinks in the same direction. Changing direction and switching to a different way of thinking is symbolised by the act of putting on a different-coloured hat, either literally or metaphorically.

A group of Year 6 pupils looking at the influence of the Beatles may use De Bono's six-hat framework to support their enquiry (see Table 5.6).

Table 5.6   Enquiry question: were the Beatles the most influential pop group of the last century?

Red hat: feelings and emotions	What is my personal view?
	What impact do I feel the Beatles had on pop music?
White hat: information and facts	What do I know about the Beatles?
	What do I need to find out?
Yellow hat: strengths and good points	What are the good features of the Beatles' music?
	What were the positive effects on life of the Beatles' music?
Black hat: weaknesses and bad points	What didn't people like about the Beatles or their music?
Green hat: creativity, new and different ideas	Are there any other individuals or groups which might have been more influential on pop than the Beatles?
Blue hat: thinking	What is my position now? Where do I stand on the question?

De Bono's Thinking Hats enables teachers to plan and support children's thinking processes in a cohesive way. Table 5.7 illustrates how De Bono's 'Six Thinking Hats' can be used to plan activities to support investigations and enquiries for 'Where in the World is Barnaby Bear?', a unit of work in Key Stage 1.

Table 5.7 Planning a Key Stage 1 unit of work, 'Where in the World is Barnaby Bear?'

De Bono hat	Activities
WHITE HAT: information *Facts; questions.* *What information do we have/need?*	• Ask the children to create a fact file about the places Barnaby Bear visits. List the name of country, capital city, major rivers, highest mountains, surrounding seas, flag, etc. • For each place Barnaby Bear visits, ask the children to compile an alphabet list/word wall/alphabet grid reflecting what each place is like (physical and man-made features, weather, etc.). • Make an A–Z zigzag alphabet book.
RED HAT: feelings *Emotions; intuition; hunches.* *No need to justify the feelings.* *How do I feel about this now?*	• Look at the photograph of traffic in a busy street, e.g. O'Connell Street ('Barnaby Bear goes to Dublin'). How would Barnaby Bear (you) feel trying to cross the road? • Look at a photograph of a busy pedestrian street. Remember, Barnaby Bear is very small, adults appear very big to him. In the role of Barnaby Bear, describe how you think he would feel if he got lost. What would he do? How do you think he would feel when he was found? How do you think his dad felt when he realised Barnaby Bear was missing and then when he was found? • Finish this sentence: 'Barnaby Bear and I felt really great when . . .'
YELLOW HAT: strengths *Good points. Why is this worth doing? How will it help us? Why can it be done? Why will it work?*	• 'Barnaby Bear goes to the Seaside.' Ask the children to look at holiday images found in tourist brochures. Use the images to list some of the good points of some of the places and things tourists do. What images do holiday brochures not show? • Why does Barnaby Bear find that flying to . . . is a better option for him than other forms of transport? • List the advantages of understanding how to behave as a good tourist.
BLACK HAT: weaknesses *Bad points. Caution; judgement; assessment. What are the weaknesses? What is wrong with it?*	• List the reasons why having a holiday at a seaside resort in the UK may not be a good idea. Then list all the advantages. • List the disadvantages of having a holiday abroad. • In groups, ask the children to word shower (brainstorm) the behaviour of a 'good' holidaymaker and a 'bad' holidaymaker. Prepare lists of such behaviours. As a class, compare lists, then ask each pupil to draw a cartoon strip which shows examples of good and bad behaviours by holidaymakers.

Table 5.7 continues overleaf

GREEN HAT: creativity *New/different ideas.* *Suggestions and proposals.* *What are some possible ways to work this out? What are some other ways to work the problem out?*	• On a postcard-sized piece of card, ask the children to draw Barnaby's favourite view of the place he is visiting. • Develop a dance based on the River Liffey ('Barnaby Bear goes to Dublin') or a piece of music based on crossing the English Channel on a very stormy day ('Barnaby Bear goes to Brittany'). • Make a healthy lunch for Barnaby Bear to pack in his rucksack for a walk up a mountain or a day out. • Make a representation/collage of or write a poem or song about one of the places Barnaby Bear visits. • Ask the children to help Barnaby Bear pack his rucksack with the things he is going to need for a day visit to the Outdoor Activity Centre in a woodland setting. • Ask the children to design a rucksack that is comfortable for Barnaby Bear to carry. Ask the children to think about the different materials a rucksack can be made of and the amount it has to hold. Test some materials for strength and for being waterproof ('Barnaby Bear to the Rescue').
BLUE HAT: thinking *Organisation of thinking.* *Thinking about thinking. What have we done so far? What do we do next?*	• What have we learnt about . . . Which different ways of learning did you find useful? • Plan a visit to . . . for your class. This unit of work uses some of the Barnaby Bear big books (published by the GA) and also on CD-ROMS (available from the GA).

There are many thinking skills activities to support learning and enquiry in the humanities. An exciting activity which always hooks the children into the learning and creates an enthusiastic buzz is the 'collective memory' or 'map from memory' activity. This activity encourages your children to think about how to work effectively as a team and how they take in and process information. The focus of the activity can be a body of text, a diagram, a map, tables and charts or a combination of these, and should represent an important element of the curriculum that you would like them to remember, for example, how life changed in the period 1950 to 2000 or a map of the locality children are studying.

Try this activity

Collective memory activity

Ask the children to work in teams of five (four team members and one observer). Each team operates as a 'human photocopier', reproducing information as accurately as possible. The team have to work co-operatively together, so developing a variety of teamwork skills.

Instructions

1. Introduce the idea of working together as human photocopiers.
2. Each team member is given a number from 1 to 4, with one observer.
3. The map or diagram to be 'copied' is placed under a sheet of paper so that you, the teacher, can reveal it easily to a small group without it being seen by the others, for instance on a flip chart turned away from the class.
4. Explain that you will call up all the number 1s and they will have a certain number of seconds to 'scan' and memorise the information. They will return to their teams and begin the process of reproducing the map or diagram as exactly as possible. Then you will call up the 2s, then the 3s, and then the 4s. Everyone will get (at least) two turns.
5. Allow time at the beginning for teams to plan how they will go about the task.
6. Start the 'photocopiers'.

Provide time for a progress review and response

Part way through, provide time for teams to reconsider and amend their strategies. Also provide time for the observers to give their feedback, so that teams have the opportunity to respond and change the way they are working.

The Thinking Skills approach tries to tackle issues of underachievement, of low self-esteem and of limited skills of social interaction. The strategies aim to promote co-operative learning (teamwork) and effective class discussions, to increase motivation and self-esteem, and support children (*and teachers*) in talking and thinking about learning. Children can be encouraged to reflect on what and how they learn, and how these skills can be applied to different subjects including the humanities, different issues and problems and real-life situations. An attempt at developing progression in thinking skills, based on Victorian Essential Learning Standards 2007, VCAA, Australia, is illustrated in Table 5.8. Further use of thinking skills and graphic organisers in enquiry in history and geography can be found in Chapter 8.

Table 5.8 Progression in thinking skills, information derived from the Victorian Essential Learning Standards 2007, VCAA, Australia

Key concept/skill	>>>>>>>> Progression >>>>>>>>		
Reasoning, processing and enquiry: Questions/enquiry	• Use the teacher's, their own or peer questions when seeking information	• Develop own questions as a guide for investigation	• Use a range of question types, including more complex questions, when undertaking enquiries • Use relevant skills and strategies from across the curriculum
Reasoning, processing and enquiry: Managing information	• Collect information from a range of sources, e.g. observations, data from own investigations • Question the validity of sources • Apply thinking strategies and tools, which might be suggested by teachers, to organise information	• Collect relevant information from a range of sources, both primary and secondary, to begin investigations • Distinguish between fact and opinion • Make judgments about the value and relevance of evidence	• Locate and select relevant information from varied sources including quantitative and qualitative • Identify and synthesise relevant information and consider its validity
Reasoning, processing and enquiry: Problem solving	• Use thinking strategies to organise their approach to problem-solving activities	• Use information they collect to solve problems	• Complete activities focusing on problem solving which involve an increasing number of variables and solutions
Reasoning, processing and enquiry: Decision making	• Provide reasons for their conclusions	• Use information they collect to inform decision making • Develop reasoned arguments using supporting evidence	• Complete activities focusing on decision making which involve an increasing number of variables and solutions • Consider own and others' points of view when evaluating evidence
Creativity: Generating ideas	• Apply creative (hypothetical) ideas in practical ways	• Use creative (hypothetical) thinking strategies in a range of contexts	• Apply creative thinking strategies to explore possibilities in a range of contexts

Creativity: Generating solutions	• Use open-ended questioning and integrate available information to explore ideas, experimenting with a range of creative solutions	• Generate imaginative solutions when solving problems by working with both concrete and abstract ideas (their own and those of others)	• Generate multiple options, problem definitions and solutions
Creativity: Testing and exploring ideas	• Test the possibilities of ideas they generate	• Test the possibilities of concrete and abstract ideas (or processes) generated by themselves and others including the unfamiliar	• Demonstrate creativity in the ways they engage with and explore ideas
Reflection, evaluation and metacognition: Using the language of thinking	• Use appropriate language to explain their thinking	• Articulate their thinking processes by using appropriate language	• Use specific language to describe their thinking
Reflection, evaluation and metacognition: Evaluating effectiveness	• Identify strategies to organise their ideas • Identify and provide reasons for their point of view	• Use a broad range of thinking processes and tools and reflect on and evaluate their effectiveness	• Explain the purpose of a range of thinking tools and use them in appropriate contexts • Modify and evaluate their thinking strategies
Reflection, evaluation and metacognition: Examining change	• Justify changes in their thinking	• Document changes in their ideas and beliefs over time, demonstrating understanding	• Describe and explain changes that may occur in their ideas and beliefs over time, when reviewing information and refining ideas • Use specific language to reflect on the thinking processes used during their investigations

Philosophy for Children (P4C)

Philosophy for Children (P4C) and the Community of Enquiry puts enquiry at the very core of education. It is a methodology for developing thinking skills, reasoning, self-esteem, respect and collaboration. It has been taken up by some schools as a method to help children engage with and confront increasingly difficult and controversial issues, through discussion and improving speaking and listening.

P4C promotes a forum for open dialogue in which children not only exchange ideas and opinions but also ask searching questions, scrutinise arguments and explore alternatives. P4C provides a safe environment in which all members are listened to and valued. It helps develop reasoning and reflection. P4C helps to build the confidence of the less self-assured to express their emerging ideas and theories and challenges the more confident to listen to and hear the thoughts and opinions of others. The process is multifaceted and profoundly personal. It presents not only an intellectual challenge to those involved but also a social and emotional one.

P4C can support the enquiry approach in humanities, as both involve generating questions, suggesting hypotheses, giving reasons and examples, making distinctions and connections, and analysing implications. Effective, collaborative group work encourages pupils to talk and discuss, giving children a safe area to in which exchange, compare, test and share their ideas with others, articulate points of view, defend their own thinking and probe the thinking of others.

A thought-provoking and very popular book that can be used as a stimulus to generate questions for P4C and also as a start for geographical enquiry is *Window* by Jeannie Baker. This book has links across the curriculum with language and literacy, global citizenship, sustainable development and interdependence. Jeannie Baker's website is listed under 'Useful websites' at the end of this chapter.

Window is a wordless pictorial story of the changing view from a window. The reader looks through the same window, on a boy's birthday, year after year for 20 years, watching as the environment changes through the impact of humans. The scene changes from natural habitat and wilderness to a rapidly expanding, polluted, overcrowded city. At the end of the book, the boy is grown up and has his own child, and we see the whole cycle of human encroachment onto wilderness area beginning again.

Possible starter questions to engage the children include:

- Where is this place?
- What do you think is happening?
- Why do you think it is happening?
- Identify the changes in the illustrations, looking closely for differences.
- What do you think it would be like to live in such a place?
- What are the similarities and differences between the first and last spread?

When *Window* was used with children (CDEC, Developing Global Learning, 2010: 17), the enquiry questions or P4C questions which the children shared included the following.

- Why does time go by so fast?
- Why are we all so motivated by money?
- Why don't people take care of the world?
- How can the world change so quickly?
- Why do humans wreck the world?

Historical and geographical enquiry

Geography develops children's knowledge of people and places and helps them understand the physical, social and economic forces that shape those places and the lifestyles of the people who live there. History by definition carries with it a temporal, time-based component. It encourages children to become explorers of the past, scrutinising the past, finding out how people lived, and provides opportunities to compare and contrast and to examine how and why things have changed, so referencing the past to our present, modern-day life, with potential implications for the future.

Although possibly not immediately recognised, history has a spatial element as well. The events, people and places of history all have a 'where', (geography). Also, geography has a temporal dimension (a history). How and why has this placed changed? An example of a whole-school enquiry which links time (history) and the spatial dimension (geography) is illustrated in the following planning, 'Holidays – past, present and future'.

Whole school planning, Holidays – past, present and future how have holidays changed since Victorian times?

Key Stage 1: Victorian seaside holidays
Enquiry: How did a typical trip to the seaside in Victorian times differ from that of today? What were holidays like in Victorian times?

Children have the opportunity to investigate seaside holidays using artefacts and picture evidence from both the Victorian period and today.

- Suitcase containing images and photographs from today and from Victorian times, and real and replica seaside souvenirs and mementos. Ask the children to sort and compare.

- Ask the children to use the images and photographs to help them put the objects they are handling into context.

- Children play traditional seaside games, sing songs, etc.

Children generate their own subsidiary enquiry questions, such as: How did people get to the seaside resort? Did they swim in the sea? What were bathing machines? Who used bathing machines and why? What is a pier? What is a promenade? When were postcards first sent?

Key Stage 2, Years 3 and 4: holidays, 1950–1970
Enquiry: What were holidays like between 1950 and 1970?

- Invite a senior citizen (grandparent or great-grandparent) into school to talk to the children about their memories of seaside holidays, covering topics such as food (for example, picnics, fish and chips, candyfloss, ice cream, rock, etc.); entertainment (such as donkey rides, boat trips, shows at the end of the pier); clothes and swimwear; beach games and fun (buckets and spades, sandcastles, ball games); travel to their seaside location (train, bus, car, etc.); pocket money; fairgrounds; souvenirs and where they stayed (caravan, chalet, holiday camp, hotel, etc.).

- Ask the children to think of some questions to ask the visitor about their childhood holidays, such as: Where did you go on holiday? How did you get there? Where did you stay? Did you swim in the sea? What games did you play on the beach? Did you watch Punch and Judy? Did you walk along the promenade? Did you walk along the pier? What sort of food did you eat? What did you wear on the beach? What sort of souvenirs did you buy?

Key Stage 2, Years 5 and 6: holidays from 1970
Enquiry: What changes in holiday destinations took place in the 1970s and why (for example, fall in the price of air travel, allowing more people to travel abroad)?

- Where did people start to go for their holidays?
- Why was it easier to get to these places?
- What have been the positive and negative impacts of mass tourism (that is, package holidays) to places like the Costa del Sol?

Enquiry: What other types of holidays, beside holidays to the sea and sun, have become popular since the1970s (for example, holidays to mountainous regions for winter sports)?
  Children generate their own subsidiary enquiry questions, such as: Why are tourists attracted to mountains? Why has sport-based tourism boomed over the past 30 years? What type of mountain activities can you do in winter/summer? Why do some mountains and villages depend on tourism? What are the advantages of tourism to mountainous areas? What are the disadvantages of tourism to mountainous areas?

Key Stage 2, Years 5 and 6: holidays now and in the future
Enquiry: What is a 'staycation'?
  Children generate their own subsidiary enquiry questions, such as: Why have 'staycations' become more popular since 2008?
  Enquiry: What is eco-tourism? How can I become an eco-friendly tourist?

- Ask the children to design a checklist or top ten tips on how to be an eco-traveller.

- Ask the children to plan an eco-friendly family holiday to Egypt for two adults and two children. Include in the visit the following: Mum wants to see the pyramids and have a sail on the River Nile. Dad and one of the children want to go scuba-diving to see the wonderful coral and exotic fish in the Red Sea. Younger brother/sister wants to have a ride on a camel, play in the warm sunshine on the beach and swim in the sea. Prompt the children to consider carefully the hotels to stay in (thinking about the hotels' 'green/environmental' policies), the food and meals, the guides employed, the transport used, how to behave as a tourist, etc.).
- Ask the children to write a menu for lunch, using locally produced food.
- Ask the children to design and label an Egyptian Red Sea eco-friendly hotel.

Different ways to end your enquiries in history and geography

There are many different creative and imaginative ways children find to present their discoveries at the end of an enquiry. Some enquiries require straightforward presentations of written reports, *PowerPoint* presentations or oral presentations, etc. Other enquiries result in some very innovative and ingenious displays and presentational methods.

- Children produce their own newspaper reports or role-play a TV news programme with presenter, roving reporters, experts giving opinions, etc.
- Children develop their own class museum, for example, Life in Britain during the Second World War or an art exhibition on the theme of the life and wives of Henry VIII.
- Children may become experts on a subject such as pollution, climate change or natural disasters and use hot seating and role-play to present their findings at a 'world' conference.
- The children produce a TV sports report such as 'Medals galore at the ancient Olympics'.
- Children design, make and display a Viking longship. Children create information cards that tell others about the Vikings, their ships and why they were greatly feared.

- Children prepare and take part in a Roman banquet. Ask one group of children to become famous chefs and prepare food for a Roman banquet. Ask a second group to make costumes for it, another group to design the invitations and a fourth group to prepare Roman entertainment. All enjoy the banquet!

- Children, using movement, dance and music, enact the eruption of a volcano (some children are the core, others the mantle and melted rock, others the crust).

- Children design an ideal holiday environment for a particular purpose, such as for a wheelchair user.

- Children develop an area of the school grounds following an enquiry, such as which seeds to plant in the school sensory garden. This follows work on the types of plants that meet their group's criteria (for example, colour of flower, scent, texture, culinary use, etc.).

- Children write and present a group piece of music that describes a storm, how a storm grows from silence, becomes violent and dies down again. Children select the best instruments to represent the sounds of the storm.

☐ Summary

It is through enquiry in history and geography that children learn to think like a historian or a geographer and this influences the way they view their world. The enquiry approach puts the pupil at the heart of the learning process, building on their prior knowledge, developing their curiosity and helping them to make sense of the world (past, present and future). The teachers are facilitators of this learning.

Good enquiry questions in the humanities spark the children's imagination and sense of wonder. Therefore, the effective use of open, probing questioning is at the core of the enquiry approach and underpins the whole of the teaching and learning process. In the humanities the questions Who? What? Where? How? When? Why? are the basis of enquiry.

Thinking skills and strategies are essential tools that support enquiry. Thinking is a social activity and children need time to think, discuss and reflect. Thinking frames help scaffold the promotion of thinking skills and enable children to deal effectively and creatively with the enquiry or problem to be solved.

References

Blooms, B.S., Engelhart, M.D., Furst, E.J., Hill, W.H. and Krathwohl, D.R. (1956) *Taxonomy of educational objectives: the classification of educational goals; Handbook I: Cognitive Domain*. USA: Longman.

Cheshire Development Education Centre, Developing Global Learning (2010) *Think Global through P4C*. Chester: CDEC.

De Bono, E. (1992) *Teaching Your Child to Think*. London: Penguin.

DfEE/QCA (1999) *The National Curriculum Handbook for primary teachers in England*. London: DfEE and QCA.

DfES (2005) *Key Stage 3 National Strategy*. London: DfES.

Higgins, S., Baumfield, V. and Leat, D. (2001) *Thinking Through Primary Teaching*. Cambridge: Chris Kington Publishing.

Jackson, E. (2000a) *Barnaby Bear goes to Dublin*. Sheffield: Geographical Association.

Jackson, E. (2000b) *Barnaby Bear goes to Brittany*. Sheffield: Geographical Association.

Jackson, E. (2000c) *Barnaby Bear and the Badger Tunnel*. Sheffield: Geographical Association.

Jackson, E. (2001a) *Barnaby Bear to the Rescue*. Sheffield: Geographical Association.

Jackson, E. (2001b) *Barnaby Bear at the Seaside*. Sheffield: Geographical Association.

Jackson, E. (2003) *Barnaby Bear goes to Norway*. Sheffield: Geographical Association.

Leat, D. (1998) *Thinking Through Geography*. Cambridge: Chris Kington Publishing.

Martin, F. (2006) *Teaching Geography in Primary Schools. Learning to Live in the World*. Cambridge: Chris Kington Publishing.

Nichols, A., Kinninment, D. and Leat, D. (2001) *More Thinking Through Geography*. Cambridge: Chris Kington Publishing.

Pohl, M. (1997) *Teaching Thinking Skills in the Primary Years (A Whole School Approach)*. Australia: Hawker Brownlow Education.

Pohl, M. (2000) *Learning to Think, Thinking to Learn (Models and Strategies to develop a Classroom Culture of Thinking)*. Australia: Hawker Brownlow Education.

Simon, H.A. (1996) *Observations on the sciences of science learning*. Paper prepared for the Committee on Developments in the Science of Learning for the Sciences of Science Learning: An Interdisciplinary Discussion. Department of Psychology, Carnegie Mellon University.

Storm, M. (1989) 'The five basic questions for primary geography', *Primary Geography 2*: 4–5. Sheffield: Geographical Association.

 ## Websites

Victorian Essential Learning Standards (2007) VCAA, Australia: http://vels.vcaa.vic.edu.au/

National College for School Leadership: www.ncsl.org.uk

Jeannie Baker is the author of numerous picture books, many focusing on geographical and environmental issues: http://www.jeanniebaker.com

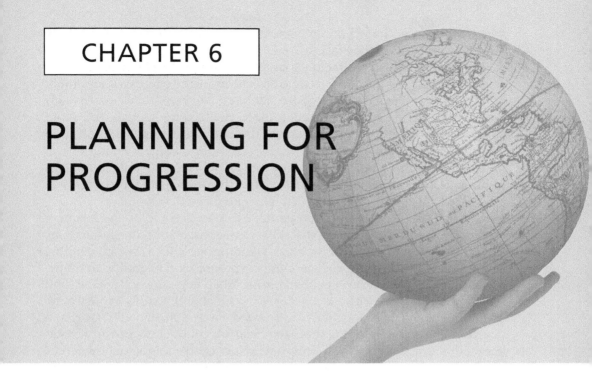

CHAPTER 6

PLANNING FOR PROGRESSION

By the end of this chapter you will be able to:

- explain progression in enquiry in terms of children's increasing participation in the process;
- use planning frameworks to plan for progression in historical and geographical enquiries;
- describe some alternative structures for the enquiry process.

Careful planning underpins all good-quality teaching. In the context of enquiry-based approaches, planning may take different forms from those used for more didactic methods, but it is no less important. Crucial to the planning process is an understanding of progression in enquiry; how teachers can ensure through their planning that children engage in progressively more challenging enquiry processes and move forward in the development of their enquiry skills. How might historical and geographical enquiries be planned to meet the learning needs and interests of children of different ages and abilities? Is there a progressive sequence of processes and experiences that children should encounter through the primary school, from Foundation Stage to Year 6?

Progression in historical and geographical enquiry could be analysed in several ways. At a simple level, it could be in terms of the contexts and content that children investigate and explore. Children will respond to increasingly more sophisticated questions, using more challenging sources and more complex data, as they progress through the primary school. The tools used for interpretation will become progressively more complex. Enquiries will gradually and progressively demand more sophisticated understandings of human motivations and physical relationships. Chapter 5 provides age-related examples of enquiries which illustrate these developments.

Such analyses have value, but together can lead to complex and adaman-tine frameworks or schemes of skills, knowledge and understandings through which children must progress. Planning becomes a time-consuming and tedious process. Effective planning for progression in enquiry requires more manageable constructs that ensure that key concepts, ideas and skills are developed, without placing unreasonable demands on teachers' commitment and planning time in a crowded curriculum. It could be argued that planning and enquiry are mutually exclusive constructs – enquiry-based learning is, fundamentally, a child- or learner-centred approach, whereas planning is essentially a teacher-centred activity. Such an argument is plainly specious, but it does point towards a more useful analysis of progression and how to plan for it.

 To think about

The enquiring learner

Although it is rather an industrial analogy, it is sometimes useful as primary teachers to think about the 'products' we want to produce at the end of the primary phase in Year 6. Essentially, what kind of learners do we want Year 6 children to be? What knowledge, understanding and skills do we want them to have at the end of seven-plus years of education? What values and attitudes to learning do we want them to display? To what extent do we expect them to be independent and autonomous learners?

With a partner, identify the key attributes you would want Year 6 to display in relation to enquiry-led learning in history and geography. Think about raising questions. Think about the sources and resources you would want children to confidently use. What tools for interpretation and analysis should they be familiar with? In what ways should they be able to confidently communicate? What about evaluation?

Now take one of these attributes and track back to Foundation Stage and Year 1. Outline how you would facilitate children's progression through to Year 6. For example, if you want Year 6 children to be able to raise their own enquiry questions in the context of a theme or a period or a locality, what experiences of question raising do they need in Year 1, in Year 3, in Year 5?

You will undoubtedly find this to be a challenging activity! Progression is essentially a very simple idea – it's about how children get better at doing stuff – but planning for progression is complex and demanding.

If enquiry is a learner-centred approach (the term 'child-centred' has certain negative connotations associated with discovery-based approaches, so is avoided here), then progression can be analysed and planned in terms of learners' progressive involvement and participation. Children will learn to do enquiry by taking on more responsibility and control over the process. In her seminal book *Learning through enquiry* (2003), Margaret Roberts produced a framework to analyse what she called the participation dimension of geographical enquiry (Table 6.1). Although the framework aims to describe types or categories of enquiry in a secondary school geography context, it provides a useful starting point for consideration of issues of progression and planning in geography (and history) at any level.

The framework can be seen as both simplistic and sophisticated at the same time. The enquiry process is represented by four stages: Questions; Data; Making sense of data; and Summary. Learners' participation in these stages (and the content explored by the process) is then categorised as Closed, Framed or Negotiated. At a simplistic level, the enquiry process is presented as a narrowly defined investigation of data – obviously appropriate to some geographical contexts, but not an accurate reflection of all geographical (or historical) enquiries – and the three categories provide a three-stage progression from teacher-led activities to learner autonomy. The value of the framework, and its potential as a planning tool, lies not in the apparently rather rigid vertical categories, but in the progressions represented horizontally across the framework.

Roberts acknowledges that the categories 'oversimplify the many ways in which teaching and learning styles can differ from lesson to lesson even with the same teacher and the same class' (2003: 35). She goes on to suggest that 'more often all three styles are used at different stages of an investigation' (2003: 36). This provides a clear clue as to how the framework can be used to plan for progression. Young children are likely to begin their experience of enquiry through the teacher-led activities described by the Closed category, but if progression is to take place, they will not stay at this level. Moving children on to a Framed enquiry process would seem the logical next step, but it is unlikely that children would gain a great deal from being moved in one step from a position of teacher dependency to a framed autonomy. Instead an element or elements of the Framed style of learning can be inserted into a Closed enquiry process so that children's learning combines the familiar with a new level of challenge. This supported or scaffolded learning (see Chapter 1 for an exploration of the theory on which this is based) is likely to be more productive and will lead on to further integration of Closed and Framed elements in subsequent enquiries, until a fully Framed enquiry process is encountered.

Likes and dislikes with Year 1:

A Year 1 teacher used Roberts's framework to plan a local enquiry with her class. Their initial experience of enquiry had been an entirely teacher-led investigation into road safety issues in the school's locality. As an extension of the project, the class addressed the question: 'What do we like and dislike in our locality?' The children went on a walk along a teacher-selected route and recorded their ideas using digital cameras, audio recorders and simple field sketches at points chosen by the teacher, including a small park with a play area, a parade of shops and an abandoned building site. Back in the classroom, the class shared their data in small group discussions and in a structured whole-class plenary. They voted to identify the most liked and disliked feature. Although much of the process was still quite Closed and teacher-led, the children were allowed to summarise their findings and present their own conclusions, giving a first experience of a more Framed approach, when drawing conclusions and reporting back.

Table 6.1 The participation dimension in geographical enquiry

	<------- Closed-------	--------Framed-------	--------Negotiated-------->
Content	Focus of enquiry chosen by teacher.	Focus of enquiry chosen by students within theme (e.g. choosing which volcano to study).	Student chooses focus of enquiry (e.g. choosing which less economically developed country to investigate).
Questions	Enquiry questions and sub-questions chosen by teacher.	Teacher devises activities to encourage students to identify questions or sub-questions.	Students devise questions and plan how to investigate them.
Data	All data chosen by teacher. Data presented as authoritative evidence.	Teacher provides variety of resources from which students select data using explicit criteria. Students encouraged to question data.	Students search for sources of data and select relevant data from sources in and out of school. Students encouraged to be critical of data.
Making sense of data	Activities devised by teacher to achieve predetermined objectives. Students follow instructions.	Students introduced to different techniques and conceptual frameworks and learn to use them selectively. Students may reach different conclusions.	Students choose their own methods of interpretation and analysis. Students reach their own conclusions and make their own judgments about the issue.
Summary	The teacher controls the construction of knowledge by making all decisions about data, activities and conclusions.	The teacher inducts students into the ways in which geographical knowledge is constructed. Students are made aware of choices and are encouraged to be critical.	Students are enabled, with teacher guidance, to investigate questions of interest to themselves and to be able to evaluate their investigation critically.

Source: Roberts (2003)

As a framework for secondary geography, Roberts's work has limited relevance and applicability to primary enquiries (or historical contexts), but could form the basis for a more primary-focused structure. In her book *Teaching History in Primary Schools* (2008), Pat Hoodless provides a similar framework as an analysis of teacher- and child-centred (her term) approaches in a primary history context (see Table 6.2). Although the focus of the framework is on quite generic strategies and a rather rigid Introduction/Task/Plenary structure (Hoodless acknowledges the influence of Literacy and Numeracy 'Hour' structures on teaching and learning in all subjects), the horizontal rows provide clear outlines of progression in children's participation in enquiry-led learning. The five vertical categories (compared to three in Roberts's framework) provide a more detailed and subtle analysis of levels of participation.

Table 6.2   Teacher-led and child-centred approaches

Teacher-led <--->				Child-centred
Teacher exposition, through storytelling, scene setting, explanation, etc.	Teacher-led question and answer.	Teacher's knowledge of children's interests and experience used to set tasks.	Teacher consults children on their interests and negotiates tasks.	Children choose their own topics for study.
Teacher-designed task for children to complete.	Teacher-designed task for children to complete.	Children carry out teacher's tasks, but with some autonomy.	Children engage in agreed research or tasks.	Children engage in individual research.
Teacher summary of what has been achieved during the lesson.	Teacher leads feedback session, to which children contribute.	Children feed back within a structure set up by the teacher.	Children create presentations with teacher support to feed back to the class what they have learned.	Children create their own presentations to feed back to the class what they have learned.

Source: Hoodless (2008)

Like Roberts, Hoodless proposes that the framework depicts a more fluid approach to teaching and learning than is at first apparent. She suggests that teachers may foster children's independent learning by adopting more learner-centred approaches in later lessons/activities within a topic or enquiry – 'teacher-led activities would predominate at the outset, with a gradual increase in the amount of child-centred, personalised learning as the children gain confidence' (2008: 47). Progression in participation, therefore, could occur in medium-term as well as long-term contexts; in sequences of lessons or activities as well as across key stages. Although both frameworks clearly show progression in participation, their value as planning tools is limited.

The framework below in Table 6.3 is based on Roberts's and Hoodless's work, but some key adaptations and changes have been made to (a) locate it more clearly in the context of primary education, (b) make it applicable to both geography *and* history and (c) make it more useful as a tool for planning for progression in children's participation in enquiry-led learning. Like Roberts's framework, there are three labelled categories of participation and one of Roberts's labels is used: Framed. The term Focused is used instead of Closed as it has less didactic connotations and better conveys the active nature of an enquiry process – although teacher-led, Focused enquiries will require children to be active, engaged learners, not just passive recipients of teacher-knowledge. The term Facilitated is used to describe the most learner-centred category because, at a primary school level, it is unlikely that enquiries will reach a stage of being entirely negotiated between teachers and learners – instead, when working with the most experienced and confident learners, the teacher is likely to take on the role of facilitator: providing resources, giving guidance and coaching, but not leaving children to their own devices. That is not to say that negotiation between teachers and learners is an unattainable goal in the context of the primary school; it is the desirable and logical aim for all who seriously intend children to become independent and autonomous learners. For planning purposes, however, this framework provides a progression for children's participation in primary enquiries, which balances challenge and achievability. In terms of labels, it must also be conceded that it is also satisfyingly alliterative!

Table 6.3 Progression in the participation dimension of enquiries in history and geography in the primary school

	<--------- Focused---------		----------Framed ---------		-------Facilitated ----->
Content	C1 Focus of enquiry chosen by teacher.		C2 Teacher's knowledge of children's interests and experience used in choice of enquiry focus.		C3 Focus of enquiry chosen by children within a given theme or topic.
Questions	Q1 Enquiry questions and sub-questions chosen by teacher.		Q2 Teacher devises activities to encourage children to identify questions and/or sub-questions.		Q3 Children devise questions within a given theme or topic and plan how to investigate them.
Sources and data	S1a All sources and/or data chosen by teacher. Sources and/or data tend to be presented as authoritative evidence.	S1b All sources and/or data chosen by the teacher, but not presented as authoritative evidence. Children are encouraged to compare the relative value of sources and/or data.	S2a Teacher provides a variety of sources and resources from which children select information using explicit criteria. Children are encouraged to evaluate sources and/or question data with explicit teacher guidance.	S2b Teacher provides some key sources and/or data. Children are encouraged to search for other relevant sources and/or data. Children are encouraged to evaluate the sources and/or question the data independently.	S3 Children search for sources of information and/or data. They select and combine information from sources and resources. Children encouraged to be critical.
Analysis and interpretation	A1 Activities involving analysis and interpretation are devised by teacher to achieve predetermined objectives. Children follow explicit instructions and are introduced to a range of approaches and techniques for analysis and interpretation.		A2 With teacher guidance, children use a range of approaches and techniques for analysis and interpretation, with some choice within given limits.		A3 Children choose their own methods of interpretation and analysis. They are encouraged to interpolate when information and/or data is inconsistent or patchy.

	<--------- Focused---------	----------Framed ---------	-------Facilitated ----->
Drawing conclusions	D1 With teacher guidance, children reach predetermined conclusions.	D2 Children may reach different conclusions.	D3 Children reach their own conclusions and make their own judgments about the question or issue.
Organising and communicating	O1 The teacher selects the audience and presentation methods for communicating findings, conclusions and actions.	O2 Children are given opportunities for selecting the most appropriate audience and presentation methods from a limited palette of choices.	O3 Children identify an appropriate audience for reporting their findings, conclusions and actions. They choose the most appropriate presentation methods.
Evaluation	E1 The teacher provides suggestions about how the enquiry might have been carried out differently. The teacher gives feedback to children on their work.	E2 Children are given opportunities to discuss the enquiry and how it might be improved or done differently. Children have opportunities to reflect on their learning and identify next steps.	E3 Children evaluate their investigation critically. They are given opportunities to refine and improve the enquiry. They are given opportunities to self-assess, peer assess and identify next steps.

Source: based on Roberts (2003) and Hoodless (2008)

The framework identifies five stages in an enquiry process from question raising to evaluation and aims to be applicable to both historical and geographical enquiry. The identification, selection and evaluation of sources (and data in the context of some geographical enquiries) is broken down into five categories, rather than three. Crucial to development of historical enquiry skills, the five categories show clearly how bridging between the Focused, Framed and Facilitated categories can facilitate progression. The enquiry process implicit in the framework is presented diagrammatically in Figure 6.1. As we shall see later in this chapter, this is not the only form which enquiry might take in the primary school, but it does reflect a commonly agreed approach. The process is presented as a cycle, rather than a process with a clear beginning and end because, for both teachers and learners, the experiences gained and skills developed in one enquiry are likely to feed into the next in terms of increased participation and learner autonomy.

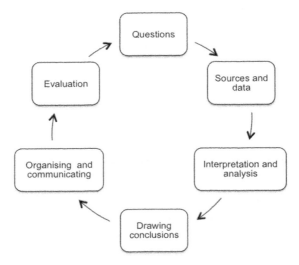

Figure 6.1 The enquiry process implicit in the progression in participation framework

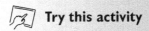 **Try this activity**

An enquiry plan

Using a blank version of the enquiry process diagram depicted in Figure 6.1, work with a partner to create an outline plan for an enquiry with a chosen primary school age range. Choose your own starting point question or try one of the following.

- How could school grounds be improved to attract more butterflies in summer?
- Why do people visit our locality?
- What are food miles and do they matter?
- Were the Romans a 'good thing' for Britain?
- Why should we be interested in the Ancient Egyptians?
- What was it like to be a servant in late-Victorian times?
- Were all Tudor kings and queens unpleasant people?

With your chosen age range, what sources and/or data would they collect? How could they interpret them? What sort of conclusions would they draw? How might they communicate their findings and evaluate?

How would sources, data, interpretation, communication and evaluation change with an older or younger age range?

The next case study provides an insight into how the framework can be used to construct and plan an enquiry in the primary history classroom. It illustrates how facilitating progression is not a simple move from one category of participation to the next. Enquiries will scaffold children's developing skills and experiences by providing familiar structures and constructs (a given theme, audience and format for communicating findings in this case) alongside new experiences and challenges (including identifying sub-questions for group investigation, evaluating the reliability of sources, improving work based on self- and peer assessment).

Victorian Britain in Year 4

Working with a Year 4 class in a large urban school, a teacher used the participation progression framework to plan an enquiry which aimed to give children some experience of a more Facilitated approach. From previous experience, he knew that the children were particularly engaged by historical enquiries that focused on the lives of children in the past of their own age (C2), so he provided a range of visual sources and simple documents relating to child labour in the early-Victorian period. Alongside printed sources, he created a simple Web page with links to Web-based information, including BBC Schools and National Archives materials. Working in groups using hard copies and a set of internet-linked laptops, the children were encouraged to identify questions and evaluate the reliability of the sources using given criteria, including questions such as 'Can we trust where this source comes from?' and 'Is the source the view of one person or more than one?' (Q2, S2a). The children were placed in mixed-ability groupings in relation to literacy skills, so that peer support would enable all children to access the written documents.

In whole-class plenary, the children shared their questions and justified their choice of sources (S2a). The teacher gave the children the task of creating group *PowerPoint* presentations about child labour (O1) which focused on conveying the everyday experiences of Victorian children to an audience of peers (children in a parallel Year 4 class). Some children were particularly interested in the role of the factory inspectors, so one group decided to create a presentation in the style of an inspector's report – as if *PowerPoint* had been available in the 1850s! Other groups responded to self-chosen questions, from the general to the more specific, including 'Was life dangerous for working children?' and 'What jobs did children do in cotton mills?'

The groups worked on the presentations on the laptops and in the school's ICT suite for two full afternoon sessions. Children were given specific roles in the groups, including 'presenter' (responsible for the design and layout of the presentation), 'archivist' (responsible for choosing the sources on which the presentation was based) and 'editor' (responsible for keeping the group focused on the question and the answers that the sources suggested). They swapped roles after given periods and were encouraged to identify key points as a group and not overload the slides (A2). The teacher maintained the focus and pace of the activity with frequent prompts and time checks. Some time at the end of the second afternoon was given over to practising and rehearsing the presentations.

Before showing the finished presentations to the parallel class, the class shared their work in plenary. Each group presented their *PowerPoint* presentation and responded to questions from the teacher and the other groups. They then went back into their groups to reflect on the experience of giving the presentation. On a simple evaluation sheet provided by the teacher, the groups elected scribes to record (a) how they could have improved their presentation and (b) which other presentation they liked best and why. After feedback in a final whole-class plenary, the groups were given a short period to make final adjustments to their presentations before presenting to their audience (E3).

At the conclusion of the enquiry, the teacher reflected on the process through discussion with the teacher in the parallel class. Although he recognised that in some elements of the enquiry he had retained control and needed to give Year 4 children more scope and responsibility (choice of content and communicating), he had successfully fostered children's question raising and allowed children to draw and communicate their own conclusions (Q2, D3). He was pleased with the evaluation process at the end of the enquiry and, although children had not had an opportunity to explicitly identify next steps, he had hard evidence on the group evaluation sheets of self- and peer assessment. Children had also had some limited opportunity to improve their work in the light of feedback from others (E3). He had plenty of information on which to base planning of the next enquiry process with the children.

Before moving on from the notion of progression in participation, it is worth noting Simon Catling's 'three Es' approach to inducting children into geographical enquiries. The approach is useful because it supplements the participation framework's learner-centred focus by emphasising changes in the teacher's role. Although not entirely compatible with the Focused, Framed and Facilitated categories of the framework, Catling's 'three Es' – Enabling, Enhancing and Empowering enquiry – illustrate how the teacher's role must change to promote and facilitate progression.

> *Enabling enquiry:* Children are inducted into an enquiry approach, drawing on their sense of exploration and inquisitiveness. While structured by the teacher to enable young children to develop a sense of focus and for ordering their enquiries, it should enable children to put forward their own questions, which they begin to investigate systematically to identify their own responses.
>
> *Enhancing enquiry:* The role of the teacher is to encourage children to take an increasing level of responsibility for identifying the questions to investigate, within a disciplined framework. The teacher challenges the children's questions and approaches, to focus them consistently on matters of geographical relevance, in relation to places, the environment and environmental spatial understanding.
>
> *Empowering enquiry:* Children are encouraged to take direct responsibility for identifying, refining, using and evaluating their enquiry questions and process. This is not only about children structuring the way they work to an increasing extent, but also about them selecting their approaches and methods and identifying with their teacher their needs, to be able to achieve the challenge they set themselves. Their teacher continues to act as a critical mentor.
>
> (Catling, 2003: 164–210)

Catling's analysis would probably not recognise the Focused category as being enquiry at all and begins with children identifying their own questions, which are then investigated with a degree of independence. Although the status of Focused enquiries might be open to debate, the value of Catling's approach is the onus it places on the teacher in terms of actively prompting and challenging children's questions and chosen approaches. At the Empowering level, the teacher's role is far from hands-off – the term 'critical mentor' suggests (Catling and Willy, 2009: 68) that the teacher should be taking on an active analytical and modelling role. As learners gain independence and autonomy within the enquiry process, the teacher's role does not lessen, but becomes more subtle, complex and challenging. An understanding of the principles of enquiry – particularly the characteristics of historical and geographical enquiries discussed in Chapter 2 – will be crucial.

Finally, in this section, an obvious question about progression in terms of participation in enquiry needs to be addressed: At what ages should children experience the different categories of enquiry in the participation framework? It would be easy to dodge this question with generalisations and platitudes about different levels of experience and development making age-specific recommendations impossible. Instead Table 6.4 attempts to link the progression to age ranges in the primary school using the codings from Table 6.3. The caveats about applying levels of participation generically to age ranges must be recognised, however, and this progression is presented as a suggested strategy for whole-school development that is open to discussion and debate.

Table 6.4 A suggested age-related progression in participation in the enquiry process

	Foundation Stage/Y1	-->Y2----->Y3---->Y4--->		Y5-------->Y6----->	
Content	C1	C2		C3	
Questions	Q1	Q2		Q3	
Sources and data	S1a	S1b	S2a	S2b	S3
Analysis and interpretation	A1	A2		A3	
Drawing conclusions	D1	D2		D3	
Organising and communicating	O1	O2		O3	
Evaluation	E1	E2		E3	

Alternative models of enquiry

Alongside participation by learners in the enquiry process, another aspect of progression will be experience of different types of enquiry processes. Figure 6.1 may be a commonly used process, but it is not the only way to

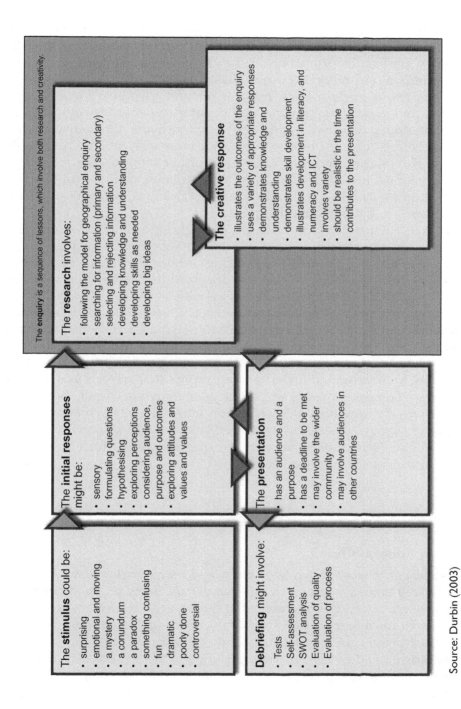

The **enquiry** is a sequence of lessons, which involve both research and creativity.

The **research** involves:

- following the model for geographical enquiry
- searching for information (primary and secondary)
- selecting and rejecting information
- developing knowledge and understanding
- developing skills as needed
- developing big ideas

The creative response

- illustrates the outcomes of the enquiry
- uses a variety of appropriate responses
- demonstrates knowledge and understanding
- demonstrates skill development
- illustrates development in literacy, and numeracy and ICT
- involves variety
- should be realistic in the time
- contributes to the presentation

The **initial responses** might be:

- sensory
- formulating questions
- hypothesising
- exploring perceptions
- considering audience, purpose and outcomes
- exploring attitudes and values and values

The presentation

- has an audience and a purpose
- has a deadline to be met
- may involve the wider community
- may involve audiences in other countries

The **stimulus** could be:

- surprising
- emotional and moving
- a mystery
- a conundrum
- a paradox
- something confusing
- fun
- dramatic
- poorly done
- controversial

Debriefing might involve:

- Tests
- Self-assessment
- SWOT analysis
- Evaluation of quality
- Evaluation of process

Source: Durbin (2003)

Figure 6.2   A model for geographical enquiry

carry out an enquiry and there are other models that may be applicable to particular content, questions, sources and/or stages of development. Two models that merit consideration for particular purposes are those suggested by Chris Durbin (2003) and Steve Pratchett (2008).

Durbin's model reflects concepts and skills from secondary geography, but has two elements which make it relevant to primary enquiries in history and geography: stimulus and creative response. Durbin suggests that children's question raising will be particularly productive if they are presented with a stimulus, which may be unconventional but should always be engaging and provocative. He further proposes that, alongside a conventional research-based phase in an enquiry, children should have opportunities to respond creatively to the questions, perceptions and/or hypotheses that the stimulus has produced.

Durbin is particularly enthusiastic about the use of images to prompt enquiry questions and the next Case Study ('Ruby Bridges in Year 2') is a brief description of a history-based enquiry where the starting point was a thought-provoking image. As already discussed in Chapter 2, imagination and creativity are fundamental to historical enquiry and can add significantly to particular geographical enquiries, especially those which focus on distant locations and future developments. Durbin's creative response is linked to this innate creativity required by some enquiries, but is focused more on creative products generated by the enquiry process, which may draw on skills, knowledge and understandings from other subjects and areas of learning – literacy, numeracy and ICT are mentioned specifically, but artistic and expressive responses will also be relevant. Creative and cross-curricular approaches are discussed in Chapter 8. The case study 'Roman Britain with Year 3' gives a brief description of creative responses which arose from another history-focused enquiry.

Ruby Bridges in Year 2

As part of her school's key stage planning, a Year 2 teacher was required to teach a unit about a famous person. Based on the interests and needs of her class, she wanted to choose a character that the children could relate to easily and a story which addressed some diversity issues. She decided to focus on the story of Ruby Bridges, the six-year-old African American girl who was the first black child to go to an integrated school in New Orleans in 1960. Every day for the first year of her school life Ruby faced an angry, baying crowd of white parents who wanted to retain the segregated schools they were used to. US Marshals guarded Ruby every day and her walk to school was famously captured in a painting by the artist Norman Rockwell called 'The Problem We All Live With'. The teacher used this image to prompt and provoke children's questions – the painting is widely available as a digital image on the Web, but the version she chose was that available in the collection on the Norman Rockwell Museum website: www.nrm. org.

Children's questions ranged from 'Who is the girl?' to 'What are the men around her doing?' to 'Who has thrown stuff at the wall?' Through discussion and voting, the children selected the questions that most interested them and the teacher used a range of resources to help them find answers, including extracts from a filmed drama about the events on YouTube and Ruby's answers to questions on her website: www. rubybridges.com. In a plenary session at the end of two lessons, the teacher engaged the children in structured discussion and an activity about the words that best summed up Ruby's character, including brave, strong, peaceful and patient. In groups, the children wrote letters to Ruby, sent as e-mail messages, justifying their choice of key word. The teacher also took an opportunity in a regular circle time session to let children share the feelings and emotions that the story had engendered. Although for the most part a Closed enquiry, the project successfully engaged children's interests and promoted some thoughtful responses because of the initial engagement with a striking and provocative stimulus.

Roman Britain with Year 3

A Year 3 teacher planned a unit about Roman Britain centred on her class finding answers to the question: 'What did the Romans do for us?' She wanted the unit to develop some research skills and also make links to Art and Design Technology. Over several lessons, children carried out research in groups about preselected aspects of Roman culture and legacy, using a range of sources, including a day visit to the Grosvenor Museum in Chester. In a plenary session, children reported their findings and were then given an opportunity to decide what they would like to make to communicate their findings to a wider audience: a wall and table display in the school's entrance hall and a class assembly. After some guided discussion, the children identified products they would like to make and spent two Roman Afternoons practising, designing and making.

The finished display contained the following products as creative responses to the question:

- a working model of a Roman ballista, which fired a 'rock' made of modelling clay at a Celtic rampart (made of lolly sticks!);
- a paper and card mosaic, showing a Roman feast;
- a model of a Roman central heating system, or hypocaust, made from clay columns and tiles;
- a model of a Roman villa, with roof tiles made of corrugated card;
- a short video on DVD in which a child, taking on the role of a TV reporter, interviewed others (also in role and in togas!) about Roman achievements in Britain.

Although closely guided by the teacher, this enquiry had Framed elements which allowed the children to draw their own conclusions and communicate in different, quite practical ways.

Steve Pratchett (2008) proposes a different model of enquiry, which links to a key aspect of enquiry-based learning that can be easily ignored if progression focuses entirely on children's participation in the process of skill development: the importance of emotional, as well as intellectual, engagement in learning. Elements of Pratchett's work are recognisable – Awareness or question raising and Analysis are two familiar stages in his model – but Evaluation and Participation are given equal weight. For Pratchett, the Evaluation stage of an enquiry is the point at which children should engage emotionally with the issue they are investigating and explore attitudes and values. Knowing the original context for Pratchett's model – Education for Sustainable Development, or ESD – gives greater sense to his proposal, in that ESD is not just concerned with developing knowledge and understanding about the environment, but working actively to protect and improve it sustainably. Children should not only know about the environment, but also engage emotionally and feel strongly about issues and changes. Through this engagement, they move meaningfully into the Participation stage (note: not the same type of participation discussed earlier in this chapter) where they actively engage in actions to protect or improve the environment.

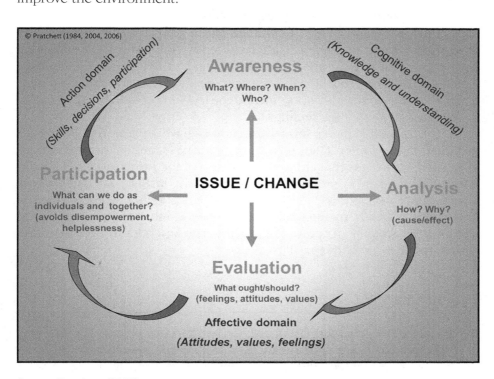

Source: Pratchett (2008)

Figure 6.3 A curriculum model for Education for Sustainable Development

It is relatively easy to see how Pratchett's model could be easily adapted and used to help in the planning of an environmentally focused geographical enquiry – for example, caring for and improving the local environment has been a key part of the primary geography curriculum for some years. Developing emotional literacy is an important part of geography – teachers need to build in opportunities for children to share their feelings about the unfairness, inequalities and environmental degradation that they will encounter when exploring a range of localities and issues. But are emotions a part of historical enquiry? The answer has to be yes, in that history is about human experiences and motivations in which emotions play a powerful role. Children will also respond emotionally to the historical characters they encounter, such as the experiences of a Victorian factory child or the behaviour of Henry VIII, and enquiry-based learning should give space and scope for feelings to be shared. In 2007, the Historical Association produced the T.E.A.C.H. report on Teaching Emotive and Controversial History 3–19 and concluded that 'emotional engagement is a feature of effective teaching' (Historical Association, 2007: 4). If children are going to persevere with the hard thinking and problem solving required by some historical enquiries, then they need to care about the people and situations they encounter. The Ruby Bridges case study describes an enquiry focus and process where emotional engagement is important and the teacher provided opportunities for children to share their feelings.

Durbin's and Pratchett's models of enquiry have a place in planning for progression in enquiry. Their relative complexity suggests that they may be alternative structures that children at the top of the primary school should encounter. As can be seen from the case study on Ruby Bridges in Year 2, this is not necessarily the case and teachers should use their growing knowledge of children's interests, learning needs and confidence to decide if alternative enquiry structures are appropriate and relevant when dealing with particular content, regardless of age.

☐ Summary

In conclusion, this chapter has focused on planning for progression in terms of children's participation in the enquiry process and also considered some models of enquiry which may be appropriate in particular circumstances. It has attempted to avoid an atomistic approach to progression, which separates out the development of individual skills and sub-processes, in favour of a more holistic dimension that considers children as participatory learners. Such an approach, hopefully, makes issues of progression accessible and manageable.

References

Catling, S. (2003) 'Curriculum contested: primary geography and social justice', *Geography*, 88(3): 164–210.

Catling, S. and Willy, T. (2009) *Teaching Primary Geography*. Exeter: Learning Matters.

Durbin, C. (2003) *Planning for the Global Dimension in Secondary Geography*. Available from the Teach Global website: www.teachandlearn.net/teachglobal

Historical Association (2007) *T.E.A.C.H. A Report from The Historical Association on the Challenges and Opportunities for Teaching Emotive and Controversial History 3–19*. Available from the Historical Association website: www.history.org.uk/resources/resource_780.html

Hoodless, P. (2008) *Teaching History in Primary Schools.* Exeter: Learning Matters.

Open University (2003) *Teach Global.* Available from the Teach Global website: www.teachandlearn.net/teachglobal

Pratchett, S. (2008) *A Curriculum Model to Underpin Education for Sustainable Development.* Available from the ESCalate Education for Sustainability and Global Learning website: http://esd.escalate.ac.uk/gattegno

Roberts, M. (2003) *Learning through Enquiry: Making sense of geography in the key stage 3 classroom. Sheffield*: Geographical Association.

 Websites

Key sources in relation to Ruby Bridges are:

Rockwell, N.P. (1894–1978) *The Problem We All Live With* [painting]. Available from: http://collections.nrm.org

Ruby Bridges LLC (2004) *Ruby Bridges Official Website.* Available from: http://rubybridges.com

CHAPTER 7

LEARNING THROUGH ASSESSMENT

By the end of this chapter you will be able to:

- identify generic definitions and features of good practice in assessment;
- begin to understand the philosophy and ideologies underpinning assessment purposes and forms;
- identify different forms of assessment and contexts in which they might be appropriately deployed;
- identify some key strategies for future practice, taking into consideration potential constraints and opportunities;
- feel more confident in promoting learning through assessment in humanities education.

Introduction

Assessment is a broad term which applies to a number of discipline-related contexts. A generic definition of assessment is fundamentally about the classification of someone or something with respect to its worth; a judgment about the value of a person or thing.

Within the field of education there are a number of ways in which the term 'assessment' is defined. This is in part due to the variety of contexts and purposes of assessment within which different forms and strategies might be deployed. As with many aspects of learning and teaching, what is pivotal is to ensure that assessment is used appropriately and effectively. It is crucial to be able to recognise and evaluate variation in practice and to understand the complexity in terms of the impact on learning and development. A key and fundamental consideration is about 'fitness for purpose'; when it is most appropriate to use specific assessment techniques with a view to complementing rather than contradicting learning. Assessment is not a 'bolt-on'; it should be an integral part of sound pedagogy within an enquiry-based approach.

What are the features of good practice in assessment?

The structure of this chapter has been deliberately sequenced so as to start by drawing on your own knowledge and experiences of assessment, both as a learner and as a teacher or trainee teacher. Assessment is a complex and diverse area to explore, with schools and institutions developing their own policies and practices. For a deeper understanding of assessment which will help you to apply key principles within different contexts, it is helpful to think about generic definitions and features of good practice before moving on to subject-specific examples. The underpinning ideologies and purposes of assessment alongside the various forms it may take are key elements to take into account when planning for assessment for learning. As the chapter progresses, there will be increasingly more humanities-specific examples included, so as to illustrate basic models and techniques which are consistent with enquiry-led learning. As a leader of learning, it is critical that you develop your confidence in relation to this important area.

To think about

Features of good practice in assessment
Assessment is a process which is:

Empirical

Informative

Developmental

Evaluative

Transparent

Fair

Rigorous

Sustainable

Engaging

Motivating

Dynamic

Put the above into a rank order and justify your choices. Identify any features you think might be missing and consider whether there is any form of progression or chronology which might help you to implement these.

Table 7.1 Features and related characteristics of good practice in assessment

Feature of assessment practice	Characteristics	Example within historical enquiry	Example within geographical enquiry
Empirical	Consequences or evidence which can be observed or experienced	Record of how well children can order a sequence of historical events on a timeline with chronological accuracy	Record of how children use question stems to raise and note geographical questions around a photograph of a location or feature
Informative	Something which provides useful information	Analysis of children's accounts of an event or famous person which they have worked on independently using a number of sources	Analysis of children's sketch maps of a river system drawn and labelled independently in the field

Developmental and dynamic	A significant and positive event or change	Use of empirical and evaluative evidence collected during the school year to identify future needs (next lesson, next term, next year) in terms of chronological understanding	Use of empirical and evaluative evidence collected during the school year to identify future needs (next lesson, next term, next year) in terms of locational frameworks
Evaluative	A process whereby the value or worth of something might be ascertained	Analysis of children's mind maps about life in the Roman Empire when using sources within *an enquiry-based context, with and without mediation by a more expert adult or peer*	Analysis of children's mind maps life in India and Asia when using sources within *an enquiry-based context, with and without mediation by a more expert adult or peer*
Transparent	Open and easy to see through and understand	Consultation with children about expected outcomes (what they need to show and do well) in response to a recent museum visit. For example, chronological accuracy and an understanding of similarities between 'then and now'	Consultation with children about expected outcomes (what they need to show and do well) in response to a recent topic on their own local area. For example, within the context of a tourist guide, children need to include a map with accurate use made of co-ordinates, symbols and a key
Rigorous and fair	Accurate and thorough methodology which is free from bias	Analysis of pupil response to task involving deductions made from a set of sources about life in Victorian times; formulation and sharing of objectives with the class prior to the lesson	Analysis of pupil response to task involving inferences made from data collection by pupils when investigating their local river; formulation and sharing of objectives with the class prior to the lesson
Engaging and motivating	Attracting attention in a way which is motivating to improve performance	Sharing of assessment information in relation to a topic on Aztecs or a locality in Kenya within the context of a dialogue with the child. Identification of strengths ('Best Work' file as selected with children) and scaffolding target setting with children for future humanities topics in a way that is meaningful, achievable and motivating	
Sustainable	Having a continuing and lasting effect	Track the assessment data as described above and develop systems of monitoring and also of reporting so that children know when they have achieved a specific target and can think about future areas of development	

Philosophy: who is it for?

As your own personal philosophy about learning, teaching and assessment evolves, one of the key questions you will be grappling with is, who are some of these processes and procedures in education actually designed to serve? This is particularly relevant when considering the purpose of assessment.

 To think about

Think about assessments undertaken by yourself as a learner and children in your class.

How is that assessment information used?

Where is it reported?

Who is the audience?

Which types of assessment do you feel helped you most as a learner and why?

Which types of assessment do you think are most helpful for children in your class and why?

Forms and purposes of assessment: how and for whom?

The two main forms of assessment comprise summative assessment and formative assessment. While distinct, the two are not necessarily mutually exclusive.

Summative assessment is, as the name suggests, a summary of achievements, often in the form of a score, percentage mark or alphabetical grade. It is usually indicative of where an individual (or group of individuals if the work is collaborative) has reached in terms of learning and achievement. It is a valuable form of data for external agencies who may be evaluating the effectiveness of programmes and the institutions who deliver them. For example, within a school context, standard assessment tasks and tests (SATs) identify which level children are working at in preparation for key transition points such as between key stages and age phases.

Formative assessment is more centrally concerned with feedback which will enhance future learning, performance and attainment. It is characteristically representative of a dialogue between teacher (or a more expert other) and learner. This may be in written form or shared verbally. For example, within further and higher education contexts, often students will be given written feedback which accompanies a grade or mark and often key development points are cited. Importantly, however, formative is not always formal and very often refers to the process of questioning and mediation which can happen in learning contexts across all ages. Think back to Chapter 1 and the explanation of Vygotsky's Zone of Proximal Development.

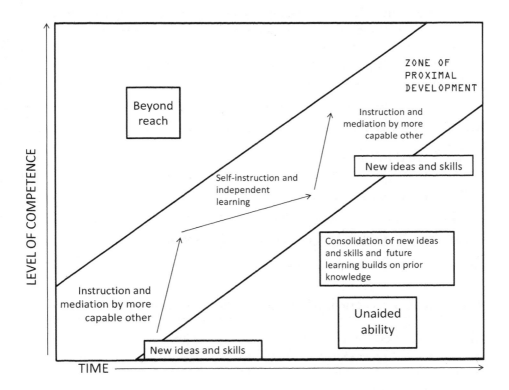

Figure 7.1   The Zone of Proximal Development

To think about

Thinking about the middle band, which represents the positive correlation between time and competency, what are the key factors here in terms of progress and how does this relate to assessment?

Can you locate the opportunity for formative and summative within the context of this diagram and where the two may overlap?

Can you identify some *humanities-specific* examples of less formal and more formative methods of assessment with a focus on questioning and mediation?

Can you identify some *humanities-specific* examples of more formal and summative methods of assessment with a focus on identifying progress and higher levels of achievement?

Now think back to earlier thoughts about assessments undertaken by yourself and learners in your class.

To think about

Why do we assess learning?

Who do these different forms and types of assessment serve and why?

How does this relate to the individual and to society?

Assessment in practice: what do we assess and when?

Having identified different forms of assessment and who these might serve, the next critical aspect is the ability to identify what to assess and when. This is of particular significance for the humanities, where time is a constraint, but given that children have the right to progress and achieve in all subjects, not just the core.

Think back to Chapter 1 where Blooms et al.'s taxonomy of cognitive domains was explored.

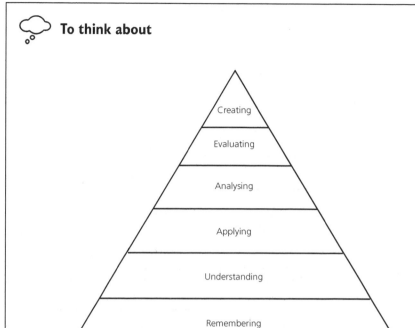

To think about

Figure 7.2   Taxonomy of cognitive domains
Source: Based on Anderson (2001) after Blooms et al. (1956)

Given the hierarchy suggested by Blooms et al. and Anderson, in terms of assessment, should this determine levels of thinking assessed?

Do 'lower levels' of (for example) 'remembering' only apply to the youngest children, with older children in Key Stage 2 being more likely to give a creative response? Think about key aspects of historical and geographical enquiry such as chronological and locational frameworks.

A taxonomy like this is often used with 'gifted and talented' children to ensure that provision is challenging enough – do you think all children (irrespective of age and ability) should have the opportunity to exercise these cognitive domains and be assessed in doing so?

Below are annotated examples of historical enquiries where all domains feature within the enquiry. It is argued that this is possible at both key stages and even with the youngest children.

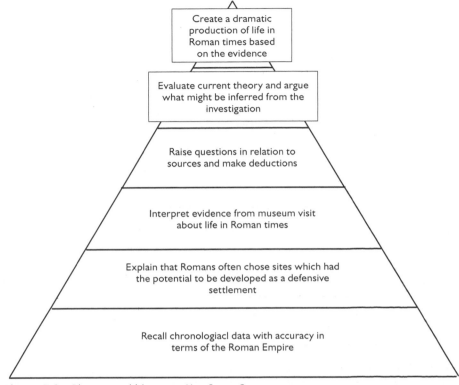

Figure 7.3   Blooms and history at Key Stage 2

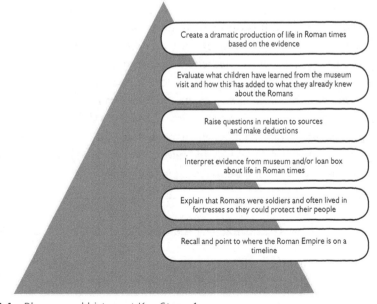

Figure 7.4   Blooms and history at Key Stage 1

Looking back to Chapter 1, where this was first mentioned, a model first proposed by Roberts (2003) was identified as being very useful in terms of identifying different types of enquiry. The framework is based on a 'participant dimension' and this has been further developed in Chapter 6 so as to directly relate to historical and geographical education within the primary phase. The model is useful as it takes into account the importance of instruction and more didactic methods which are critical in terms of effective learning and teaching (see Figure 7.1 above). It also helps to emphasise that enquiry takes many different forms and is certainly not restricted to work in the field or with objects (Garner, 2007). It represents a model of differentiation and progression in learning and as such, lends itself also as a framework for assessment (see Table 7.2 and also Chapter 6).

Table 7.2 Progression and assessment in the participation dimension of enquiries in history and geography in the primary school (based on Roberts, 2003 and Hoodless, 2008)

	<---------- Focused----------	----------Framed ---------	--------Facilitated ------>
Content	*C1* Focus of enquiry chosen by teacher.	*C2* Teacher's knowledge of children's interests and experience used in choice of enquiry focus.	*C3* Focus of enquiry chosen by children within a given theme or topic.
Assessment opportunities	*AsC* Children's prior knowledge assessed at start of an enquiry; development of ideas measured in a similar way at the end of the topic. *Mind and concept mapping*		
Questions	*Q1* Enquiry questions and sub-questions chosen by teacher.	*Q2* Teacher devises activities to encourage children to identify questions and/or sub-questions.	*Q3* Children devise questions within a given theme or topic and plan how to investigate them.
Assessment opportunities	*AsQ* Children's responses to questions set and their ability to identify their own appropriately focused questions at the outset *Ongoing interactive 'Working Wall' of questions identified by all*		

Table 7.2 continues overleaf

	<---------- Focused----------	----------Framed ---------	---------Facilitated ------->		
Sources and data	*S1a* All sources and/or data chosen by teacher. Sources and/or data tend to be presented as authoritative evidence.	*S1b* All sources and/or data chosen by the teacher, but not presented as authoritative evidence. Children are encouraged to compare the relative value of sources and/or data.	*S2a* Teacher provides a variety of sources and resources from which children select information using explicit criteria. Children are encouraged to evaluate sources and/or question data with explicit teacher guidance.	*S2b* Teacher provides some key sources and/or data. Children are encouraged to search for other relevant sources and/or data. Children are encouraged to evaluate the sources and/or question the data independently.	*S3* Children search for sources of information and/or data. They select and combine information from sources and resources. Children encouraged to be critical.

AsS

Assessment opportunities

Children's use and evaluation of sources and resources within the enquiry
Class 'Enquiry Diary (Part 1)' where sources used are reviewed and evaluated by class members throughout the year for all humanities topics

Analysis and interpretation	*A1* Activities involving analysis and interpretation are devised by teacher to achieve predetermined objectives. Children follow explicit instructions and are introduced to a range of approaches and techniques for analysis and interpretation.	*A2* With teacher guidance, children use a range of approaches and techniques for analysis and interpretation, with some choice within given limits.	*A3* Children choose their own methods of interpretation and analysis. They are encouraged to interpolate when information and/or data is inconsistent or patchy.

AsA

Assessment opportunities

Children's choice and use of techniques of analysis and interpretation
Class 'Enquiry Diary (Part 2)' where techniques of analysis and interpretation are reviewed and evaluated by class members in relation to different types of enquiry questions throughout the year for all humanities topics

	<---------- Focused----------	----------Framed ---------	---------Facilitated ------->
Drawing conclusions	*D1* With teacher guidance, children reach pre-determined conclusions.	*D2* Children may reach different conclusions.	*D3* Children reach their own conclusions and make their own judgments about the question or issue.
Assessment opportunities	**AsD** Children's ability to draw conclusions with and without scaffolding by the more expert other *Ongoing monitoring of conclusions and responses to enquiries using a post-it system to identify children who exceed or fall short of expectations*		
Organising and communicating	*O1* The teacher selects the audience and presentation methods for communicating findings, conclusions and actions.	*O2* Children are given opportunities for selecting the most appropriate audience and presentation methods from a limited palette of choices.	*O3* Children identify an appropriate audience for reporting their findings, conclusions and actions. They choose the most appropriate presentation methods.
Assessment opportunities	**AsO** Children's ability to identify purpose, presentation methods and audience as fitting for focal enquiry *Class 'Enquiry Diary Part 3' where a palette of presentation methods is annotated for future reference*		
Evaluation	*E1* The teacher provides suggestions about how the enquiry might have been carried out differently. The teacher gives feedback to children on their work.	*E2* Children are given opportunities to discuss the enquiry and how it might be improved or done differently. Children have opportunities to reflect on their learning and identify next steps.	*E3* Children evaluate their investigation critically. They are given opportunities to refine and improve the enquiry. They are given opportunities to self-assess, peer assess and identify next steps.
Assessment opportunities	**AsE** Children's ability to reflect on their own learning and identify recommendations for the future *Children list 'Five Golden Rules' for anyone undertaking a similar enquiry and for their own use in the future*		

Assessment in practice

Table 7.2 details a range of foci and strategies for assessing children at different points within the enquiry cycle.

 To think about

As a teacher, how would you plan for assessment across the different stages of each enquiry within history and geography?

Would you use the same pattern of assessment for each enquiry or might the focus shift during the course of the school year?

Bear in mind that many assessment strategies are identified within Table 7.2 and, depending on the enquiry focus and purpose of assessment, you may be selective about which stages you decide to assess each time.

What sort of evidence would you keep and how would you use it?

How are you going to celebrate achievements and share feedback with children?

Consider the strengths of peer assessment (for example, the 'Enquiry Diary' and 'Five Golden Rules') and take into account relevant research that suggests the potency of this in terms of future learning and progression.

How will you effectively share what it is you want the children to achieve?

 To think about

Ask your peers, colleagues or children to draw a diagram of a house and state that you will be marking these pictures out of ten.

When drawings are complete ask peers, colleagues or children to swap theirs with the person next to them, as they will be marking it against criteria which you share at this point:

1. windows and a door (2 points)
2. front garden (2 points)
3. window boxes (2 points)
4. driveway (2 points)
5. cat on the windowsill (1 point)
6. curtains (1 point)

What scores were achieved and what issues are raised?
Recent research indicates that transparency in terms of specific assessment criteria and expectations around general issues such as presentation need to be shared with those being assessed.

Some of the issues raised above, including use of evidence, giving feedback, the role of peer assessment and improved transparency, have been considered in Table 7.3 by practitioners who developed this very useful matrix.

 To think about

Table 7.3   Assessment for learning techniques within the context of lesson planning (based on work by Kate Donovan and the PGCE Primary Group, University of Chester, 2011–12)

Learning objectives (and assessment criteria where appropriate)	Success criteria
• Share all Learning outcomes/ assessment criteria with the children as appropriate • Clearly relate outcomes to the age/ key stage of the children and make the terminology child friendly • Ask children to write the outcomes/ criteria on their whiteboards and in their own words • Set learning objectives in line with National Curriculum but also tie in what the children want to learn (as is consistent with an enquiry-based approach) • Map out objectives and criteria on whiteboard at the beginning of the enquiry (like a learning journey), e.g. objectives – description of lesson – key questions children should think about • Outcomes and success criteria are fundamental to the lesson and as such you need to make sure they are at the forefront of your mind when planning: what am I aiming to achieve by doing this?	• Must, should, could at beginning of the lesson • Pupil self-assessment against the success criteria at end of the lesson • With framing and facilitation consistent with an enquiry-based approach, ask children to help in setting the success criteria, thinking about prior knowledge and areas of interest • Instead of telling the children what you are looking for, show them. Modelling is key to success and consistent with what Vygotsky said about scaffolding within the Zone of Proximal Development • Show a good example, telling the children what makes it good • Make success criteria achievable and ask children if they want to add any (negotiated outcomes giving children further responsibility)

Questioning

- Understand when it is appropriate to use open-ended and closed-ended questioning within a framed enquiry and in particular when introducing and using sources and resources (remember Blooms et al.'s taxonomy and the hierarchy of cognitive domains – which are more closed and which are more open?)
- Have a class 'Question box' where children can select questions stems and types to help shape their own historical and geographical enquiry
- Integrate key questions within medium- and short-term planning, leaving room for contributions from pupils as appropriate
- Get children to ask questions of other children, perhaps when showing an example of their work or how they have completed a particular activity
- If a question comes up that you had not expected or that is unusual, make it into an enquiry – 'we'll come back to that' – perhaps make it the problem of the week
- Ask further questions and think on your feet; if children ask questions that you do not expect, respond to them with a further question and make it a two-way dialogue
- Ask children what they want to learn about a particular topic and post their questions in a box, perhaps at the beginning of the topic, and then post all the questions and further related questions up onto a 'Working Wall' as the enquiry progresses

Feedback	Self- and peer assessment
• Always working towards 'closing the gap' and moving children's learning forward	• Ask children to tell you how they feel about what they have done and produced
• Target prior learning and take into account previous achievement within lesson planning; include assessment of what children understand after one lesson and what might be expected within subsequent lessons on the basis of this	• Link self- and peer assessment to the success criteria as this has potency
	• At end of lesson recap on learning outcomes and success criteria and then get children to mark their own work: 'I did this well . . . I need to work on this'
• Give feedback personally by sitting down and talking to the children (instead of just writing it in books) – 'a star and a wish'	• Ask children to traffic light their work in relation to success criteria (RED: understanding not strong, I am not confident about this; AMBER: understanding has developed but I still have questions; GREEN: I understand this)
• Ongoing verbal feedback aimed at continuously 'closing the gap'	
• Start the lesson by asking children to read feedback and respond to it, helping them to direct and take responsibility for their own learning	• Use mixed-ability grouping and peer assessment
	• To make peer assessment effective children need to be taught how to do it

Constraints and opportunities

The main constraint for those leading learning in primary humanities is time. Despite this constraint, assessment is an integral part of an enquiry-based approach. It relates closely to the learning theories identified within Chapter 1 and features strongly throughout the book in terms of examples and models cited.

Learning is a highly emotional journey and the affective dimension must be taken into account. Performance, attainment and achievement are all inextricably linked to emotions and a sense of self-worth as a learner and as a person. Children need to be clear about where they are heading and why and what they need to do to improve. In practice this is challenging, but 'do-able'. Despite the obvious time constraints, there are additional opportunities for assessing humanities content and processes across the whole curriculum and within homework and extracurricular activities.

☐ Summary

Within this chapter, generic definitions and features of good practice in assessment have been explored with a view to beginning to understand the philosophy and ideologies underpinning assessment purposes and forms.

Different forms of assessment and contexts in which they might be appropriately deployed have been identified and critiqued. Strategies for future practice, taking into consideration potential constraints and opportunities, have been identified and illustrated with reference to primary humanities.

It is hoped that by exploring the fundamental aspects of and rationale for assessment within an enquiry-based approach, you as a professional will feel empowered and confident in taking this forward to promote learning and achievement within the context of humanities education.

Further reading

The following list represents recommendations for further reading to explore assessment in generic and humanities-specific contexts.

Briggs, M., Martin, C., Swatton, C. and Woodfield, M. (2008) *Assessment for Learning and Teaching in Primary Schools* (2nd edition). Exeter: Learning Matters.

Cahn, S.M. (2009) *Philosophy of Education: The Essential Texts.* New York: Routledge.

Clarke, S. (2008) *Active Learning through Formative Assessment.* London: Hodder Education.

Curren, R. (2007) *Philosophy of Education: An Anthology.* Oxford: Blackwell.

Harrison, C., Howard, S., Black, P., Marshall, B. and Wiliam, D. (2008) *Inside the Primary Black Box* (1st edition). London: GL Assessment.

References

Garner, W.P. (2007) Unpublished thesis, available at: http://chesterrep. openrepository.com/cdr/handle/10034/97297

Hoodless, P. (2008) *Teaching History in Primary Schools.* Exeter: Learning Matters.

Roberts, M. (2003) *Learning through Enquiry.* Sheffield: Geographical Association.

CHAPTER 8

CROSS-CURRICULAR APPROACHES AND CREATIVITY IN TEACHING ENQUIRY-BASED HUMANITIES

By the end of this chapter you will:

- appreciate that cross-curricular approaches to teaching enquiry in the humanities are relevant and reflective of how children learn, and help children develop a deeper understanding of generic skills and concepts, such as learning and thinking skills, as well as predispositions relating to social and emotional aspects of learning;
- understand that stimulating, cross-curricular approaches to teaching enquiry in the humanities motivate and challenge children to learn and offer them a creative way of applying the knowledge, skills and understanding learned from other areas of the curriculum, so enabling children to make connections across the learning landscape;
- appreciate that cross-curricular approaches to teaching enquiry in the humanities are reflective of the real world, in which learning is not defined and categorised by separate disciplines;
- understand that enquiry in the humanities through cross-curricular approaches engages children's imagination and creativity and encourages them to take the initiative and be active participants.

Over the decades, there have been many debates in educational circles about the cross-curricular approach (often referred to as 'topic') versus single-subject-specific teaching. In the late 1960s, Lady Plowden stated that 'Rigid division of the curriculum into subjects interrupts children's train of thought and interest . . .' (The Plowden Report, *Children and their Primary Schools*, 1967: 197) and in 1991, Arnold wrote in *Topic Planning and the National Curriculum* about ways of organising learning through areas of learning and experience.

However, in the 1970s and 1980s, successive governments and inspection systems identified issues with learning and teaching through what they called vague, woolly and fragmented 'topic'. It was argued that many of the cross-curricular links were shallow and artificial, that the topic work was often poorly planned, not focused rigorously enough on specific subject content, skills or understanding and lacked progression and continuity. Often, much of the children's learning involved low-order skills such as copying from textbooks and colouring in pictures and maps. The progression in key skills and concepts of subjects like art, history and geography often got lost. In 1992, in *Curriculum Organisation and Classroom Practice in Primary Schools*, generally referred to as the 'Three Wise Men Report', Alexander, Rose and Woodhead demanded an increase in single-subject teaching.

From 1999, the National Curriculum insisted that children develop an understanding of the complex and diverse yet interdependent and ever-changing world in which they live: 'Education must enable us to respond positively to the opportunities and challenges of the rapidly changing world in which we live . . .' (DfEE/QCA, 1999: 10). Children need to learn about their present-day place in the world and to have an awareness of their past in order to shape their aspirations and hopes for the future.

However, in 2009, both the Cambridge and Rose Reviews recognised the need for a more thematic approach to learning. *The Cambridge Review of Primary Curriculum* (Alexander, 2009) suggested 'Time and Place' as an area of study and learning. Rose, in the *Independent Review of the Primary Curriculum Report* (Rose, 2009) advocated 'human, social and environmental understanding' as an area of learning in a proposed new curriculum. Following the publication of the above two reports, in 2010 the government of the day requested another full review of the curriculum before they recommended any particular changes in pedagogy.

Cross-curricular approaches to teaching enquiry in the humanities are reflective of the real world, in which learning is not defined, classified and pigeonholed by separate subject disciplines. A cross-curricular approach allows children to make natural connections between content areas without being limited by artificial boundaries. This supports the children in constructing their own meaning and developing the skills they will need for life in the twenty-first century.

In order to ensure that the cross-curricular approach is successful, teachers, when planning, need to understand what learning outcomes, knowledge, skills and understanding they expect to develop from the topic. They then try to make the learning meaningful by helping children connect content and skills across the curriculum. The children explore a topic from different angles, discovering the cross-curricular connections. They begin to realise that different parts of their learning journey come from different, discrete disciplines (for example, science, geography, history, English language, maths, ICT, citizenship, and art). By using content and skills from a variety of subjects the curriculum is enhanced and enriched. This helps to move learning on and reinforces what children have already learned.

In geography, the spatial aspect of a topic, children learn about places, the human and physical processes that shape them, and the people who live in them. They start with the local and move out to the global, so the skills developed through geography help children make sense of both their immediate surroundings and the wider world. They learn about the impact of human activity on the planet and understand the importance of developing a future that is sustainable.

> Primary geography is a curriculum jewel. Geography is challenging, motivating, topical and fun. In our diverse society children need, more than ever before, to understand other people and cultures. The Geographical Association believes that geographical knowledge, concepts and skills are essential components of a broad and balanced curriculum.
>
> (The Geographical Association Position Statement, 2009)

History stimulates curiosity about the past and connects the past with the present and the future, giving children a deeper understanding of themselves and others and a sense of belonging.

So, the humanities make important and unique contributions to a child's education, as these subjects are all about 'us', past, present and future, and our impact on the place where we live locally and other places globally. Geography and history are the subjects that inspire the children to think about their own place in the world, their values, their rights and responsibilities to other people and the environment. Enquiry through these subjects enables children to begin to understand how today's actions shape the future of tomorrow.

History and geography are both interdisciplinary. As Owen and Ryan (2001) indicate, the power and also the weakness of geography is that it is such a 'wide-ranging subject', dealing with many different things, places and people. When children are 'doing geography' or 'doing history' they are not doing this in isolation. Good learning, in geography and history, in the primary school both draws on and contributes to other subjects, drawing on other subjects as tools to support the humanities and contributing to other subjects as the context or topic focus.

Teachers need to explore the interrelationship of subjects. They need to organise the curriculum in creative and manageable ways and develop appropriate learning and teaching strategies which motivate and challenge children and also ensure progression in the content, skills and understanding of the different contributing subject disciplines. Strong, meaningful connections and links between subject areas leads to interesting and relevant teaching and creative, exciting and memorable learning experiences for the children. A rigorously planned and well-taught cross-curricular approach to the humanities inspires and enthuses children's imagination. The children are motivated and work with an enhanced sense of purpose and understanding.

Enquiries in history and geography engage children in real-life problem solving and require children to apply knowledge and skills from across the curriculum (maths, English, art, technology, design, music, drama and dance, PSHE, citizenship, ESD and the global dimension, etc.) Enquiry in humanities develops the asking and answering of questions, which underpin critical literacy, citizenship and thinking skills. Through enquiry, the cross-curricular links are emphasised, as the children learn more than historical and geographical skills and knowledge.

Subject skills which support enquiry in humanities

Information and Communication Technology (ICT)

ICT is a tool which can be used to support investigations and enquiries in humanities and across the curriculum. ICT, which embraces a whole raft of technologies that are broadly concerned with finding out information and communicating the results, can be used in a variety of ways. In the first place, it can be used as a reference source. For example, in history, the internet can be used to carry out research and interrogate information about historical events or famous people and, in geography, to find out facts and information about places and physical features. Second, ICT can be used to store, organise and graph data. In addition, data logging supports the development of the skills of observation, measurement, interpreting data, inference and prediction. Third, ICT can be used, in primary humanities, as a means of communication. Blogging and e-mails enable children to exchange a variety of experiences and information about their place with children from other schools, both locally and globally. Greater communication with children from other areas of the world enables children to empathise more and consider the wider implications of their actions, particularly in geographical, environmental and sustainability contexts.

Digital cameras, digital video and audio recorders may be used to record visits, places and re-enactments of historical events. Smartphones engage children and are a simple way of capturing images, videos and sounds when out and about. Some smartphones also have augmented-reality software installed to give additional information about a place viewed through the device's camera. ICT will also support the presentation of information, from simple word processing or desktop publishing through to multimedia presentations. Together, the digital camera, *PowerPoint* and interactive whiteboards have enormous potential to enhance children's learning through enquiry in primary humanities. They provide excellent opportunities for children to consolidate knowledge, assume ownership of their learning, engage in high-level critical thinking and communicate their learning to peers, teachers and wider audiences. By preparing a presentation, children are involved in communicating all aspects of planning and carrying out enquiries, rehearsing hypotheses, describing methods and discussing their recording procedures.

Language and literacy

The enquiry approach in humanities, including the use of the outdoors, visits and visitors, is a great stimulus and provides endless language opportunities, including ways to enhance speaking and listening skills. For example, the journey sticks activity, described later in this chapter, is one that clearly indicates a sequence of experiences on the journey and can provide an excellent support for retelling the journey orally or for writing stories and accounts, as well as in embryonic map making.

The enquiry approach promotes pair and small group work, giving children opportunities to learn through interacting with each other, talking and discussing their ideas and clarifying their thoughts. Through taking turns in speaking and listening to each other, and particularly in listening to the views of their peers, children start to modify and amend their own thinking.

Drama and role-play can also be incorporated into historical and geographical enquiry, for example, hot-seating a character in role in history. Through historical enquiries, children can research different aspects of the past to be used in their role-play and drama. If the role-play is to be successful, accurate and authentic, the children are required to look carefully at the evidence. The role-play then provides the opportunity for participants to explain their views, in role, to a wider audience, while the rest of the class can ask questions.

The use of secondary sources such as letters, diaries, text, maps and photographs can stimulate creative writing and writing in other genres, as well as developing historical and geographical vocabulary. Enquiries in both history and geography can deliver all the main categories of non-fiction writing genres, including instruction, recounting, explanation, information, persuasion, analysis and evaluation (see Table 8.1).

Table 8.1   Geographical enquiry questions and links to language and literacy

Key geographical question	Activities	Writing genre
Where is this place?	• Booking a holiday (use of a tourist guide/internet, etc. to plan a holiday) • Planning a journey. How to get to the place/holiday destination. What sort of transport are you going to use and why? • Planning what to take on a journey, e.g. packing a suitcase activity	*Procedure and instruction*
How do people get to the place?	• What sort of transport are you going to use to get to the place and why? Write a summary of the pros and cons of different transport methods available • Prepare a report on the public transport available in the locality	*Non-chronological report* Comparison, summary
What is this place like?	• Description of the place • Design a holiday brochure/tourist guide/'grot' spot guide	*Recount* *Non-chronological report*
Why is this place like it is? How is this place changing? Why is it changing?	• Write a report on how the place is changing • Analysis – interpreting surroundings • Research old documents. Analysing place names to discover origins of the settlement	*Report writing* *Explanation* Note taking
How do people feel about these changes?	• Empathy – interviews/debates with 'locals' in role • Design questionnaires	Questionnaires
Compare localities?	• Comparison: create a list of similarities and differences in written or pictorial form	Lists

What is the landscape like?	• Description of the landscape. Description may be written in character, e.g. a local, a tourist from another country, an elderly person, a young person, a developer, etc. • Poem describing landscape	*Recount* *Narrative* Poetry
What goods and services are available there?	• Shopping basket activity. What can you buy locally? • Create a menu, using local produce, for a restaurant/cafe	Lists Menu
What jobs/work do the adults do?	• Prepare job advertisements for one of the jobs in the area • Write a statement to put forward to local councillors giving reasons why new industries should/should not be encouraged to develop in the area • In role, prepare leaflets to persuade/ criticise/protest/support/object/ confirm the above statement	*Persuasion* *Discussion/persuasion* Writing/arguing a point of view/leaflets
Where do people live?	• Estate agency – description of houses in locality	Commentaries/persuasive
What is it like to live/work in this place?	• In role, write a diary entry for someone who works in/at . . . • Empathy: 'A day in the life . . .'	*Recount*
What is it like to visit this place?	• Diary • Write and address postcard or letter to a friend about the place you are visiting	*Recount*
What links does this place have with other places?	• Plan a visit to the next town/city/to grandparents, etc. in another part of the country or elsewhere in the world	Sequencing Non-chronological writing
What is the weather like there?	• Use weather statistics and prepare and present a weather forecast • Write a newspaper report of a disaster, e.g. 'Local river floods settlement', 'Delayed at the airport! Airport comes to a standstill because of the weather conditions/ Icelandic ash cloud' • Pack and label a suitcase for a visit to this place	*Explanation* *Report* Journalistic

Increasingly, literacy supports enquiry in both history and geography. Story and non-fiction books can be rich sources of historical and geographical information and can transport children in their imagination to different places, cultures and times. In order to be able to understand the story, knowledge and understanding of the place, the people and the time (period in history) are essential.

Stories from other cultures can be enriching, providing opportunities to celebrate the diversity of the world. In geography, children can use both non-fiction texts and also fictional stories to begin to 'identify and describe what places are like'. In history, children can begin to develop an understanding of life in a certain period of history (for example, by reading Anne Frank's diaries). Picture and illustrated storybooks enable children to imagine they are on the other side of the world or in other times during history.

Year 5 Plan. The use of a fiction book to develop enquiry through cross-curricular links – geography focus

A Year 5 teacher in a primary school in the Greater Manchester area used the fictional story 'Masai and I' by Virginia Kroll as an introduction to a unit of work on Kenya. The story offered the children a positive introduction to Masai customs and lifestyle, and excellent opportunities to explore similarities and differences between the two cultures. In the story, Linda, a young, African American girl, learns about the Masai tribe and begins to daydream about what her life would have been like if she had been born in Kenya, into this East African tribe. She compares her own urban, Western life with that of an imaginary Masai friend living in rural Kenya by thinking of all the events in a typical day.

Curriculum area	Activities/Enquiry questions based on the story 'Masai and I' by Virginia Kroll and linked to work on Kenya
Literacy and Language	Children interrogate the text, asking questions such as: • Who is telling the story? • How might this book be different if it compared the Masai lifestyle with that of an American girl living in the country; or an African girl living in an African city? • If a Masai boy or girl visited your school, what questions would you like to ask him or her? Use of words: • vocabulary: discuss the meaning of some of the words used in the story, for example, kraal; kinship; gourd • adjectives: discuss the adjectives used in the book to describe the Masai people.

Maths	Directions: • Discuss the location of different countries in Africa, using the points of the compass. Coordinates: • Use lines of longitude and latitude to describe location.
ICT	E-mail: • Exchange letters with a school in Kenya. Internet searches: • Find out information about Kenya. Word processing and presentations (PowerPoint)
Geography	Ask the children: • What do you know about Africa? • What do you think of when you hear the word Africa? Explain to the children that Kenya is one of the countries in Africa. Focus the enquiry on parallel lives – compare and contrast; similarities and differences; daily routine; food; friends; neighbours; environment; animals. Ask the children: • What kind of food do we, they eat? Where does it come from? • What do we, they use for transportation? • What is the environment, climate like in each area? • What kinds of clothing do we, they wear? • What other things live near us, them? • What are the homes and buildings like? • What kind of jobs do we, they have?
History	Because her ancestors were originally from a part of Africa, the African American girl in the story feels a certain 'affinity' and 'empathy' with the Masai people. 　　Ask the children if they feel 'affinity' or 'a bond' with any particular people. This may lead to a discussion about where their ancestors are from.
Science	Animals • Ask the children to find out about animals found in Africa: animals for domestic use (for food, clothing, transport, etc.); wild animals; animals unique to Africa; animals found in other parts of the world as well as Africa. • Ask the children to find out about animal habitats in Africa. Health • Water is essential to life. Discuss sources of water in Kenya and what water is needed for. Discuss where Kenyan people get water for domestic use. Discuss clean water, drought, sanitation, etc.
Art	• Discuss African art style and produce artwork 'in the style of' African art. • Make a Masai necklace.

Primary and secondary sources of information can be used in the literacy, as either a springboard for or to support historical or geographical enquiry. Children conducting historical enquiries using non-fiction texts are often presented with a wide range of historical sources. Through the skills of critical literacy (Table 8.2) children begin to thoroughly question the source, looking for areas of agreement or disagreement and even contradiction. Also, children develop a deepening awareness of the various viewpoints of different authors on events, as this helps them to identify bias and exaggeration when evaluating the usefulness of sources.

Table 8.2 Interrogating text in historical enquiries

Text	Usefulness for historical enquiry
Why was the text written? Purpose?	What is the source? Is it a diary entry? A letter? A textbook? An official report? Something else?
	What purpose was the source written for?
Who was the author of the source?	Who wrote it? Who produced the source?
	Was it an eyewitness? Was it a historian who has researched the event?
Type of source?	Is it a primary source from the time of an event, e.g. Samuel Pepys's diary of aspects of the Great Fire of London?
	Is it a secondary source written after the time of an event? Library book? Textbook?
Content?	What does the source tell us?
	Could it have missed out any information?
What does the text not tell you? Limitations?	What are the limits/weaknesses of the source?
	Could it be biased? Exaggerated? One-sided?
	Why is it not the perfect source?
	Could it have missed out any information?

Mathematics and numeracy

Mathematics is a tool for everyday life. It provides a way of viewing and making sense of the world. It is used to analyse and communicate information and ideas and to tackle a range of practical tasks and real-world problems. Children's learning and progress in many subjects, including enquiry in the humanities, often depends on what they know and understand and can do in mathematics. Mathematics is a language – in fact, the only truly universal language – and is also essential in fostering logical and rigorous thinking.

To think about

In a small group, discuss how mathematical knowledge, skills and understanding can be used to support enquiry in the primary humanities. Focus your thinking on the use of number, measurements and data handling.

Now read the details below, illustrating what children in primary schools are taught in mathematics focusing on (i) number, (ii) shape, space and measure and (iii) data handling. How do you think these skills can be used to support enquiry in primary humanities?

Number
Numeracy is an essential life skill; without basic numeracy skills children will be disadvantaged throughout life.

In primary school, children are introduced to whole numbers and numbers less than 0, fractions, decimals and ratios. Children learn to use and understand percentage as the number of parts in every hundred. Probability is also introduced, including the use of specific vocabulary including certain, impossible, likely, unlikely, even chance.

Shape, space and measure
In primary school, children are introduced to metric and imperial units, as appropriate, for length, area, weight, height, temperature and time. Negative numbers are also introduced, for example in temperature and also depth below sea level.

Data handling
In primary school, children are introduced to a variety of data handling methods including:

- graphs: construct, use and interpret
- bar-line graphs: represent, construct and interpret
- bar chart for categorical data: construct and interpret (for example, distinct categories such as ways of travelling to school)
- bar chart for grouped discrete data: bars are labelled with the range to represent
- line graphs – construct and interpret
- pie charts: interpret and compare; construct simple pie charts

Mathematics is embedded in most other subjects. The skills developed in maths are not ends in themselves, but tools which can be used to support investigations and enquiries in humanities and across the curriculum. Children need to develop strategies for checking their answers to judge whether they are reasonable. An understanding of the ways in which numerical information is gathered by counting and measuring and is presented in charts, tables and graphs is essential, as well as the ability to explain, interpret and make predictions from data. Mathematics is needed to make sense of and aid interpretation of historical and geographical data collected through enquiry.

At the same time, subjects such as history and geography give relevance and real-world situations and issues for using mathematics. It is through meaningful, relevant contexts, such as enquiries in history and geography, that children learn best to use, apply, practise, consolidate and extend mathematical and numeracy skills. Children enjoy and are motivated by enquiries and practical investigations. These provide the fun and excitement which help children internalise mathematical skills and so aid learning.

Geographical enquiry provides a meaningful focus and purpose for data collection, presentation and analysis. Data collection in a geographical context involves mathematical decisions, as well as geographical skills. Data representation and interpretation involves geographical judgments, as well as mathematical skills. Learning is enhanced in both the humanities and in mathematics.

Problem solving in mathematics follows a similar cycle to the enquiry cycle, as illustrated in Table 8.3.

Table 8.3   Links between problem solving in mathematics and the enquiry cycle

Problem solving in maths	Enquiry cycle
Specify problem Formulate questions in terms of data needed Decide what data is to be collected	Activating prior knowledge and experiences Creating a need to know • curiosity Establish the enquiry: develop a broad overarching enquiry question, from which children can develop subsidiary enquiry questions • estimate and speculate • hypothesise • decide on data to be collected • plan questionnaire (if relevant to enquiry)
Collect data from variety of sources including primary and secondary sources	Collect evidence and information • collect data

Process and represent data Turn raw data into usable information that gives insight into the problem	Undertake investigation and enquiries, testing hypotheses using sources • use data • sort, classify, sequence, represent data • present graphical interpretation (if appropriate)
Interpret and discuss data Answer initial question by drawing conclusion from data	Compare, interpret and analyse information making sense • analyse • interpret • reach conclusion
Evaluate results	Encourage children to • reflect on learning – reliability and validity of the data, graphical techniques used • what has been learned? • what worked and what didn't? • how could enquiry be made better? • what would they do differently next time?

Geography in particular is a numerate subject. For example, enquiries and investigations into climate and climate change involve using and understanding climate graphs, such as graphs where temperature is plotted with a line and rainfall is plotted with a bar graph. The use of co-ordinators in four quadrants is taught in the primary school, in Year 6. The location of places is given using grid references of varying complexity, depending on the age and ability of the children (see Table 8.4).

Science

As with all the enquiry-based subjects, the approaches in science are generally focused on real life. This engages the children, because they feel the work is relevant to them and is helping them develop skills that prepare

Table 8.4 Progression in geographical skills linked to mathematics

Location of places	Scale and distance
• Follow simple directions: up, down, left, right, forwards, backwards • Talk about own picture maps	• Use relative vocabulary: bigger/smaller, like/unlike
• Follow directions: use four points of a compass to follow directions (N,S, E and W) • Make a map of a short route experienced • Follow a route using a plan	• Simple scale drawings of different sizes of objects • Draw objects on a table, from a bird's-eye view, to scale using squared paper

Table 8.4 continues overleaf

• Follow directions: Use eight points of a compass to follow directions (N, S, W, E, NW, NE, SW, SE) • Co-ordinates: use letter/number co-ordinates • Ordering: draw a route, showing main features in the sequence • Use a large scale map outside	• Scale drawings of classroom, e.g. I cm reps I m; Isq cm: I sq m
• Locate places/features on OS maps using four-figure grid references • Use OS maps for routes and wider interpretation. Select maps for a purpose • Compare large scale map and vertical aerial photographs	• Measure straight line distance on a plan • Scale drawings, e.g. plan of school/school grounds • Understand what the scale actually means on OS map (e.g. 1:50,000 means Icm on the map is equivalent to 50,000 cm in real life) • Use string and the scale on an OS map to measure distances
• Use six-figure grid references to locate features on an OS map • Latitude and longitude on atlas maps as locational guides • Follow a route on a small scale map and describe features seen • Draw scale plans of increasing complexity	• Understand that scale can be shown in different ways • Compare and interpret different map scales • Understand more complex scales

them for life and citizenship in the twenty-first century; skills such as critical thinking, collaborative working, consideration of alternatives and effective communication. While the skills that can be developed through enquiry are of value, enquiry does not lead to understanding in science unless it concerns content that provides opportunity to develop scientific ideas. This is the same for other enquiry-based subjects; the content and context has to be appropriate to the focus (for example, geography or history or maths).

The enquiry-based approach in science is based on the five 'e's of the social constructivist approach: engage, explore, explain, elaborate and evaluate. This builds on children's existing knowledge and skills and synthesises new understanding from this prior learning. The children hypothesise and gather evidence through their own investigations and observations and from secondary sources. They are encouraged to think creatively, reason, explain and reflect critically on outcomes.

There are many different types of scientific enquiry, such as fair testing involving the control of variables, pattern seeking (for example, in surveys) and identification and classification.

Many topics undertaken in humanities, particularly geography, offer strong cross-curricular links with enquiry in science. Examples such as 'weather', 'climate' and 'climate change' encourage children to use information gathered through enquiry in a number of different ways. In mathematics, children learn to take weather measurements (for example, with thermometers and wind gauges) and to represent this information through diagrams, weather charts and graphs.

In geography, the children consider the spatial aspects of weather, what the weather is like in particular places and how different weather conditions affect people (for example, droughts, types of homes, clothes people wear) and impact on the environment (for example, erosion, flooding, etc.). Children explore weather patterns through enquiry in the local area; for example, which parts of the school grounds are sunny, shady, sheltered, frosty, etc. In the science curriculum, children carry out experiments and investigations as part of the water cycle (for example, evaporation and condensation of water) and in design technology, children may make weather 'measuring' instruments (such as a rain gauge, wind sock, anemometer).

Investigations into waste and reusing, reducing and recycling link geography enquiries into how to improve the local environment to science. Children, through enquiries and investigations about the production of waste in school and at home, consider ways in which the actions of individuals might help to conserve some of the earth's resources. As part of this, they may also discuss the different types of materials from which the waste is made and how different types of rubbish could be disposed of, reused or recycled. This could also lead on to investigations into the use of packaging or in siting landfill sites (waste disposal sites) and incinerators.

Subjects which enhance enquiry in humanities through the cross-curricular approach

Citizenship

Enquiry in both history and geography are closely linked to skills and understanding in citizenship. Both subjects support the development of some of the analytical concepts and personal skills of citizenship. They provide children with opportunities to practise critical thinking skills and also develop the skills of empathy with others. For example, in history, the enquiry question 'What do you think it would have been like to live in Britain during the Second World War?' could cover rationing. Subsidiary enquiry questions may include the following:

• What was rationing?
• Why was rationing necessary? Was it a good idea? Why?

- Which foods were rationed? Why? What would a family of four (two adults and two children) have to eat in one week? How would you feel if you were one of these children?
- What foods were not rationed? Where did these foods come from?
- What kind of foods do we eat today? How do they differ from the food available during the war?

These activities may involve children looking at ration books and weighing out the exact amount of the rationed food for one week, to develop an appreciation of what families actually had to live on. Children could sort food into baskets, one containing those foods available during the war and one containing those not available. They could look at wartime recipes, find out about the 'Dig for Victory' and 'Make do and mend' campaigns. From this the children are able to discuss opinions on rationing, food availability and what it would have been like to live in Britain during the war.

In geography, through enquiry at Key Stage 1, children consider 'the quality of the environment in their local street.' They may begin to consider their right to play and be safe in their local neighbourhood and who is responsible for this. They may also start to consider how their own actions could encroach on and interfere with the rights of others. The evidence, derived through the processes of enquiry, helps children to discuss and reach informed judgments about current issues, particularly local issues that directly affect them. As well as being geographical, because they have a spatial dimension, the enquiries are also the essence of citizenship, and help children to develop the confidence to take informed action.

The development of an enquiry approach through geography can provide a framework for exploring a range of local and global issues, such as pollution, the environmental impact of food miles, carbon footprints, fair trade, etc. Global themes such as interdependence, sustainability, rights and responsibilities are introduced at an appropriate level.

Personal, social and health education

As with citizenship, both history and geography have strong links with PSHE. In history, investigating the way of life of people in the past and, in geography, developing enquiries into the way of life of people in other countries help children to recognise and respect other people and their cultures and ways of life. Knowing we are all different and that we should respect these differences helps children understand that society is constantly changing and developing.

Religious Education

Again, both historical and geographical enquiry has strong links with RE. Many aspects are covered from a study of a specific place where faiths are shaping a community, as well as looking at values, attitudes and beliefs that shaped communities and places in the past.

Art

There may be many links between art and the enquiry approach in geography and history. In history, a painting may be of a famous person in history or from a particular era. In geography, a piece of artwork, sculpture or artefact could be linked to a particular culture or country. Artwork is a product of the time (when) and the place (where) it was produced and needs to be examined carefully, questioned and reflected on. Investigating social, historical or political contexts of art can bring a deeper understanding of circumstances in which it was produced. A portrait can reveal a variety of clues and ideas about the person in the portrait. It can tell us who a person was, how they lived and what they thought about themselves. It can even tell us about the painter and their life. An example of the use of a portrait to support enquiry in history is the use of the portrait of Henry VIII by Hans Holbein the Younger.

A Year 6 class was asked to consider the enquiry question 'Was Henry VIII a superman?' The children, using various sources of information, found evidence indicating Henry's various talents including being an outstanding sportsman, particularly in archery and jousting, an accomplished dancer and musician, playing the lute (guitar) and virginals (a keyboard instrument), and being a brilliant linguist, speaking French, English and Latin.

Then, as part of the enquiry, the children were asked to use the portrait to find out about Henry VIII's character and appearance. The children interrogated the portrait using a variety of questions.

- How can we tell that Henry is an important person? What sort of clothes is he wearing? Is there any evidence that shows us that Henry was a king?

- What do his facial expression, the way he is standing (pose) and holding his hands tell us about Henry?

- What is Henry trying to tell us about himself in this portrait?
- Do you think Henry really looked like this?

What the children found out: in the painting, the artist was trying, through scale and body language, to make Henry look larger than life, very confident and powerful. He is standing with feet wide apart, staring aggressively. His fists are clenched, like a boxer's, making him look very strong, aggressive and ready to fight. The colours, jewels and fabrics of his costume are rich, reflecting his huge wealth. Holbein, the artist, also made Henry's legs appear longer and possibly more muscular. The effect of this is to make his body look slimmer and more elegant.

The children also found out about the artist. Hans Holbein the Younger worked at Henry's court and was commissioned by Henry to paint his portrait. Commissioned portraits often flatter the person in them. Henry commissioned this portrait to make him look young, healthy, tall, rich, powerful and strong. The children realised that Hans Holbein wanted to keep his job and his head, so he painted a portrait to flatter Henry.

An example of creative art linked to geography and enquiry are journey sticks. Journey sticks began with aboriginal people, who put them together when they went on a long journey and then used them on their return as prompts when telling the rest of the tribe about their journey. Journey sticks are now well used in primary schools as a way of introducing maps.

 Try this activity

Journey sticks
- Introduction
  Whole-class discussion: What is a map? What are maps used for? What are the key features (title, compass direction, key or legend, scale) of a map? What experiences have children of using maps?

- Journey stick activity:
  Each pupil begins with an empty stick and as they walk around an area they collect items that interest them, attaching these in chronological order to their stick, thus marking the journey they have taken. The items are personal to each child, which encourages a sense of personal geographical experience. Children may also add stickers (emoticons) to mark emotions evoked by places on their journey.

- Map-making activities:
  Linear map: Following the journey stick completion, ask the children to make a linear map of what they found on their route. They may add emoticons to their map. In pairs, ask the children to share their linear maps. This begins the process of being aware that geography can be a personalised subject.

  Map of area: With class, discuss turning and twisting their linear map to create a map of the area. Remind children about key features of a map. Create a checklist for children to follow. Ask the children to make their final map, including a key and other features discussed.

- Plenary activities:
  Ask the children the following questions: How did the journey stick support you to make a map? Why was each map different?

Music

Music can support enquiries in the humanities. For example, 'Vltava' is a musical poem composed by Smetana. He uses the music to reflect the sounds of the river, as the arrangement describes the course of the River Vltava, the longest river in the Czech Republic, from its beginning, where two brooks, one cold and the other warm, join into one stream that flows through forests and meadows and different landscapes. At one place, a farmer's wedding is celebrated by a dance of the mermaids in the moonlight. The river then flows on, passing impressive castles and palaces on nearby cliffs. Finally, the river swirls into St John's Rapids and then widens and flows as a broad stream on towards Prague. From here, it disappears into the distance where it unites with the River Elbe.

Enquiries in the local environment or school grounds may include developing and mapping an outdoor music trail with differing instruments representing different areas. This could be one of the ways the children present their findings about the local area.

Enquiries in history may involve children researching musical instruments and/or interpreting music from a period in history.

Creativity

Creativity is often simply associated with the creative arts, art and music, but in fact, creativity permeates the curriculum and is a vital aspect of every subject. It can be seen and identified in all aspects of the arts, literacy, humanities, sciences, mathematics and technology. The National Curriculum Handbook (DFEE, 1999: 22) included creativity within the section on thinking skills. It stated that: 'Creative thinking skills . . . enable children to generate and extend ideas, to suggest hypotheses, to apply imagination and to look for alternative innovative outcomes.'

Creative learning, the cross-curricular approach, focusing on history and geography and enquiry, go hand in hand. Lloyd and Smith stated in *Developing Creativity for learning in the Primary School. A practical guide for school leaders* (NCSL, 2004), that it is possible to identify when children are thinking and behaving creatively in the classroom. They cited the characteristics of creativity as including being questioning and challenging, making connections and seeing relationships, envisaging what might be, exploring ideas, keeping options open, reflecting critically on ideas, actions and outcomes.

Through enquiry in history and geography, the children develop the key skills of learning, such as communication, information processing and reasoning, empathy, enquiry and problem solving. They are taught to be open-minded and enquiring thinkers who can transfer these skills into life and learning.

Enquiry develops the use of thinking skills, so enhancing children's learning through creativity. Pupil self-esteem is raised, as they are able to generate their own ideas and feel valued for their input.

Creativity was taught in the 1970s and 1980s, through topic-based projects. However, as indicated earlier, there was a lack of accountability, detailed planning and rigour. In the late 1980s and 1990s, much of this 'creativity' disappeared as it did not fit into the centrally prescribed National Literacy or National Numeracy strategies. Children's learning was rigidly and tightly planned by teachers following national 'guidance'. Curriculum time was squeezed, not allowing enough time for creativity or even for teaching the humanities. Teachers felt that creativity wasn't valued by central government, as success in this area is difficult to measure or put into statistical league tables.

In the late 2000s, this situation had started to change, with the acknowledgement that performance and attainment at the end of Key Stage 2 had plateaued and continual improvement wasn't going to be achieved through more of the same (that is, through more centralised prescription of how and what had to be taught).

> There is a belief that creativity for learning is not only a way of thinking and behaving, to be valued in its own right, but also a means of improving children's learning and raising standards across the whole curriculum.
>
> (Lloyd and Smith, 2004: 5)

Research into how the brain works has resulted in increased understanding of the functions of each side of the brain. Most children, as with most adults, have one side of their brain which is more dominant and which will affect their approach to learning. The left brain primarily deals with language, mathematical processes and logical thought, the traditionally more academic approach. The right brain predominantly deals with music, visual aspects and patterns. In order to maximise the potential learning of *all* children there needs to be input that appeals to both sides of the brain, for example, creative, visual activities as well as those relying on use the use of language, mathematics and logic. Humanities subjects, such as history and geography, because they synthesise material and ideas from different areas, have the potential to be highly creative subjects. It is important to recognise this and to allow time and space for creativity.

Over recent years, some teachers have indicated that children are not able to think for themselves and lack the ability to be creative. Research into how the brain works has highlighted that, when significant stress occurs, communication between the two parts of the brain, the reptilian brain (which controls the more basic thought processes) and the neocortex (which controls higher-order thinking skills and creativity) does not take place. When a pupil is placed in a stressful environment, creativity may be seriously inhibited. Many children find the 'reward and punishment', 'one right answer' and 'test'-based systems, which are used in many classrooms, very stressful, so it should be no surprise that children are not able to think and that their creativity has been stifled. Enquiry-based learning supports higher-order thinking and creativity and moves away from placing children in stressful, threatening situations.

All children learn in different ways but usually respond best to high-challenge, low-threat environments. Simple strategies adopted during the enquiry approach to learning in the humanities support many children. As an example, word showers (brainstorming) require both divergent and convergent thinking (see Try this activity). Generating new and varied ideas is a product of divergent thinking, while reducing a range of options down to the most relevant ones or a single solution is a product of convergent thinking. Word showers tend to be effective because children are free to say what they think without fear of criticism. The process encourages innovative and new ideas, building on the ideas of others, reflecting on ideas, discussing and feeding back.

 Try this activity

Encouraging creative problem solving through brainstorming or word showers

- Create a non-threatening atmosphere that is open and positive.
- Welcome all ideas.
- Ensure that no one and no thought will be subject to criticism or ridicule.
- If a pupil does not wish to contribute at a given time, this is perfectly OK.
- Everyone has the right to pass.
- Write ideas on sticky notes so that they can be moved and rearranged as desired.
- Continue the initial word shower process (brainstorming) until no new ideas are being generated.

In humanities, to maximise its potential, creativity requires careful and precise planning, with an understanding of the subject key skills to be developed, as well as the subject knowledge and content. In all subjects some skills depend on a hierarchy of learning; this hierarchy must be followed for learning to be successful. In addition to subject-based skills, key skills may also include key skills for learning, which develop the children's communication, teamwork and problem solving skills. Helping children to express their creativity through enquiry in the humanities involves providing them with opportunities to investigate the world around them, either through first-hand experience or secondary sources; to express their own ideas, and make choices and connections. Creative thinkers are able to transfer knowledge and understanding gained in one context to another.

Fostering creativity through enquiry in the humanities involves offering children 'real choices' and developing their confidence in making decisions on what to investigate, who to work with, how to conduct the investigation, and in selecting ways of communicating their findings.

Encouraging links between subjects strengthens creative learning, but care must be taken that the links are genuine and not contrived. For example, a visit to the local shopping centre can inspire work in numeracy, literacy, art, history, ICT, etc. However, if the geographical enquiry question 'How is this place connected to other places?' is not explored, then it cannot also be contributing to the children's geographical understanding of interconnectedness.

Curiosity, defined in the dictionary as 'an eager desire to know', is the starting point for learning. If children are not inspired and interested, then they won't engage. Curious children have a sense of wonder and actively explore the world around them. They ask questions about what they see and make predictions about why things happen in a particular way. They test their theories, interpret the results of these investigations and share their discoveries with others. Children's observations can be very profound at times and demonstrate deep thinking of a spiritual nature. Respecting and valuing this awe and wonder and helping children to communicate it will encourage them to be even more curious and creative.

> Creative teachers . . . need techniques that stimulate curiosity and raise self-esteem and confidence. They must recognise when encouragement is needed and confidence threatened. They must balance structured learning with opportunities for self-direction; and the management of groups with attention to individuals. They must judge the kinds of questions appropriate to different purposes and the kinds of solutions it is appropriate to expect.
> (*All Our Futures: Creativity, culture and education*,
> DfEE, 1999: 95)

When children are asked to develop a sense of place through finding out 'what is this place like', it is necessary for them to enquire what natural or cultural influences have impacted or are still impacting on the place. A wide variety of stimuli and approaches can be used including environmental awareness and developing a sense of place through identifying change over time. The use of an artist's work, like that of Andy Goldsworthy, stimulates curiosity and focuses observation skills. Music-making and role-play can engage children in developing a response to a place. Examples of creativity in history may include creating a dance that describes an ancient Egyptian ceremony or planning and running your own Ancient Greek Olympic Games.

Attitudes to learning across the curriculum

Skills can be directly demonstrated, taught and practised, but attitudes have to be fostered. The cross-curricular enquiry approach supports the developing of positive attitudes to learning and life itself. Appropriate attitudes are a prerequisite, if meaningful and in-depth learning is to take place and children are to continue to improve their attainment and performance. Essentially, a pupil needs to be enthusiastic, co-operative (within both a class and a group situation) and confident and eager to contribute questions, ideas and answers. They need to be creative and imaginative, versatile and adaptable. They need to be willing to take responsibility for their actions and to be empathetic (see matters and issues from different viewpoints). Above all, they need to be determined to succeed, and persistent and resilient when faced with a challenge or difficulties. They need support to develop coping strategies for failure and to see failure as part of the learning challenge.

Thinking skills and graphic organisers

The National Curriculum states that there five thinking skills: information-processing, reasoning, creative thinking, evaluation and enquiry skills (DfEE/QCA, 1999). These, by their very existence, are cross-curricular. There are a number of ways to support thinking skill strategies. Graphic organisers are one way for children to organise and arrange their ideas, thoughts and research when conducting enquiries, investigating or problem solving. Graphic organisers are a visual way for children to display their thinking.

They are the tools that provide scaffolding and help children track their thinking and manage, organise and record their learning. They can be used in all phases of an enquiry from word showers 'brainstorming' ideas to presenting findings.

To think about

Graphic organisers are visual frameworks that help children to:

- structure and show their thinking processes;
- organise their information, ideas and research;
- see both the whole and the parts of a problem or issue;
- plan activities and investigations;
- review and reflect on progress, understanding and skills;
- communicate effectively using images;
- extend their thinking by encouraging in-depth thought on topics and/ or issues.

(Victorian Essential Learning Standards, Australia, see website below)

In groups discuss ways in which you might use graphic organisers to support children in enquiry in history and geography.

Discuss which graphic organisers would be more supportive to some enquiries and stages in the enquiry process than others.

There are numerous different graphic organisers, too many to outline here, each supporting different aspects of the enquiry approach. Many educational websites (listed under 'Useful websites' at the end of this chapter) offer a vast range of examples of graphic organisers and advice on how to choose and best use them.

Summary

Cross-curricular approaches to teaching enquiry in the humanities are reflective of the real, complex, evolving and interdependent world in which children live. They enable natural connections between content areas to be used and developed without being limited by artificial boundaries. Learning cannot be compartmentalised into separate subject disciplines, to be taken out of the box at certain times during the school week. When children are 'doing enquiry in geography or history' they are not 'doing' this in isolation. Enquiry in history and geography emphasises cross-curricular links and develops more than just historical and geographical skills. Asking, exploring and answering of questions, the very essence of the enquiry approach, underpins critical literacy, citizenship and thinking skills. Good learning in geography and history in the primary school draws on and contributes to other subjects, both as tools to support the humanities and as aspects of the topic focus.

Planning the cross-curricular approach has to be rigorous, to ensure that the required learning outcomes, knowledge, skills and understanding are delivered and developed and that there is balance and progression across the whole curriculum.

Creativity permeates the curriculum and is a vital aspect of every subject. Strong, meaningful connections and links between subject areas leads to creative, interesting and relevant learning. History and geography have the potential to be highly creative subjects, as enquiry-based learning, the very essence of learning in the humanities, supports higher-order thinking and creativity. To teach enquiry and creativity successfully requires all the characteristics of good teaching, including high motivation, high expectations, the ability to communicate and listen and the ability to interest, engage and inspire. Techniques to stimulate curiosity and raise self-esteem and confidence are essential.

Enquiry in history and geography offers exciting and memorable learning experiences, which inspire and stimulate children's imagination.

References

Alexander, R. (2009) *The Cambridge Review of Primary Curriculum*. Cambridge: University of Cambridge Esmee Fairbarn Foundation.

Alexander, R., Rose, J. and Woodhead, C. (1992) *Curriculum Organisation and Classroom Practice in Primary Schools: A discussion paper.* London: DES.

Arnold, R. (ed.) (1991) *Topic Planning and the National Curriculum.* Harlow: Longman.

DfEE (1999) *All Our Futures: Creativity, culture and education.* Sudbury, Suffolk: DfEE publications.

DfEE/QCA (1999) *The National Curriculum Handbook for primary teachers in England.* London: DfEE/QCA.

Lloyd, K. and Smith, P. (2004) *Developing Creativity for learning in the Primary School. A practical guide for school leaders.* UK: National College for School Leadership.

Owen, D. and Ryan, A. (2001) *Teaching Geography 3–11: The Essential Guide.* London: Continuum International Publishing Group.

Plowden, J.P. (1967) *Children and their Primary Schools: Report of the Central Advisory Council for Education in England. Plowden Report.* London: HMSO.

Rose, J. (2009) *Independent Review of the Primary Curriculum.* Nottingham: DCSF.

Smith, A. (1998) *Accelerated Learning in Practice (Brain-based methods for accelerating motivation and achievement).* London: Bloomsbury.

Websites

The following educational websites offer a vast range of graphic organisers to download and print for classroom use (free of charge) and advice on how to choose and best use them.

Eduplace: www.eduplace.com/graphicorganizer/

Eduscapes: www.eduscapes.com/tap/topic73.htm

EdHelper: http://edhelper.com/teachers/graphic_organizers.htm

Education Oasis: www.educationoasis.com/curriculum/graphic_organizers.htm

Victorian Essential Learning Standards, Australia: http://vels.vcaa.vic.edu.au/support/domainsupport/thinking/organisers.html

INDEX